Yearbook of Contextual Biblical Interpretation

1 (2024)

Amsterdam University Press

Table of Contents

Introduction to the Initial Volume of the Yearbook of Contextual Biblical Interpretation 1
PETER-BEN SMIT & KLAAS SPRONK

Jesus loves me this I know, DOES the Bible tell me so? 8
SHANTELLE WEBER

Seeing and Experiencing Things Differently. How the Theologizing of Children Can Contribute to Theology 27
C.H. (CORINA) NAGEL-HERWEIJER & P.M. (RONELLE) SONNENBERG

Child Theology, Spirituality and Intersectionality 46
ANNEMIE DILLEN & AMY CASTEEL

What Hope for Children? Eschatology, the Normativity of the Future, and Christian Hope in Godly Play 57
ARMIN M. KUMMER

"Unbinding" Children's Roles in Philippine Catholic Religious Education 77
JUSTIN JOSEPH G. BADION & JULIUS ANTHONY L. PORQUERIÑO

Religion, Worldview and Diversity in School: What to Expect from Teachers? 100
DR. ERIK RENKEMA

CBI as a (Biblical Studies) Discipline 116
GERALD O. WEST

Reviews 148

Amsterdam University Press

YEARBOOK OF CONTEXTUAL BIBLICAL INTERPRETATION 1 (2024) 1-7
HTTPS://DOI.ORG/10.5117/YCBI2024.001.SMIT

Introduction to the Initial Volume of the Yearbook of Contextual Biblical Interpretation

Peter-Ben Smit, Professor of Contextual Biblical Interpretation, Faculty of Religion and Theology, Vrije Universiteit Amsterdam, p.b.a.smit@vu.nl

Klaas Spronk, Rector and Professor emeritus of Old Testament, Protestant Theological University, Utrecht, kspronk@pthu.nl

Abstract

This introduction outlines the work of the Centre for Contextual Biblical Interpretation at the Protestant Theological University (Utrecht) and the Faculty of Religion and Theology of the Vrije Universiteit Amsterdam and positions the Yearbook of Contextual Biblical Interpretation in this academic setting. After sketching the scholarly rationale of the centre, which views contextuality as a catalyst for interpretations and aligns itself with a quest for justice and the good life, the topic of the first instalment of the Yearbook and its contents are presented by outlining what a childist approach amounts to and what hermeneutical benefits it has.

Keywords: Contextual Biblical Interpretation, Centre for Contextual Biblical Interpretation, Majority Readers, Childist Hermeneutics, Innovation, Transformation

This inaugural instalment of the *Yearbook of Contextual Biblical Interpretation* is dedicated to "childist" perspectives on biblical texts. This is both of significance in and of itself, and indicative of the approach to biblical studies that the YCBI seeks to promote. This approach is in line with that of the Centre for Contextual Biblical Interpretation (CCBI) at the Protestant Theological University (Utrecht) and the Faculty of Religion and Theology (now the School of Religion and Theology in the Faculty of Humanities and Social Sciences) at Vrije Universiteit Amsterdam, which entails the conviction that contextuality is a catalyst for interpretation. The Centre particularly furthers such innovative approaches that contribute to forms of interpretation, which enhance the good life for all inhabitants of the global community, as well as beyond humankind. In doing so, the CCBI continues a longer tradition of contextual biblical interpretation in the Netherlands,[1] inspired by (Latin American) liberation theological impulses (e.g., Dom Hélder Câmara, whose name is associated with the chair of contextual biblical Interpretation at Vrije Universiteit), and locally associated with the name and pioneering work of Hans de Wit,[2] along with a number of long-standing social partners, such as the VU Vereniging and Kerk in Actie. The CCBI offers courses at undergraduate and graduate levels, contributes to continuing education (e.g, through the annual Dom Hélder Câmara Lecture),[3] hosts the annual Bridging Gaps exchange program,[4] and organizes a yearly summer school. It also conducts and facilitates a range of research projects, among which are many PhD projects,[5] frequently funded through agencies such as the Dutch Research Council (NWO), the German Research Foundation (DFG) and the European Commission's Marie Skłodowska-Curie program, in which the approaches fostered by the CCBI take centre stage.

Examples of such approaches are manifold, ranging from ecotheological work, by way of research on gender and racism, to, indeed, work on childist perspectives. Two PhD projects are currently being conducted in this field, one focused on the presence of children in the early Christian community in Corinth (Emily Plank), and one concentrating on the role of children in

1 Some programmatic output associated with this continuation is: Smit, "Contextuele bijbelinterpretatie"; Spronk, Dubbink, and Smit, eds., *Bijbel*; Spronk, Van der Ham, and Smit, "Contextual Biblical Intepretation"; Lawrence, Strømmen, Smit, and Van der Walt, eds., *Challenging Contextuality.*

2 Frequently working in cooperation (as befits the method and approach of contextual biblical interpretation), two characteristic volumes containing the output of research endeavors spearheaded by Hans de Wit are: De Wit and Dyk, eds., *Bible*; and De Wit, Kool, and Schipani, eds., *Through the Eyes of Another.* Two volumes of essays published in his honor also speak to his work and his influence: Schipani, Brinkman and Snoek, eds., *New Perspectives*; and Snoek, ed., *In Love.*

3 It has been held since 2018 and published variously, see, for instance: Noort, Hamberg, Luteyn, Van der Ham, and Smit, eds., *Bijbel*; Pruiksma, Van der Ham, Luteyn, Van Vliet, and Smit, eds., *De schepping*; Van der Ham, Pruiksma, Van Vliet, and Smit, eds., *Opstandig leven*; Sarot and Smit, eds., *De toekomst*; Punt, "Armoede".

4 On which, see: Van der Ham, Van Vliet, Spronk, and Smit, eds., *Building Bridges*; Van der Ham and Van Vliet, "Experiencing Ecumenism".

5 Completed projects include King, "The Motifs of Growth"; Furlong, "The Identification of John"; Holmgaard, "On Earth"; Troost, "Exegetical Bodybuilding"; Visser, "Perfecting Poverty"; Washam, "Regenerating the Garden"; Alkhouri, "The Kingdom of God"; Moreno Palacios, "Impacto del neopentecostalismo".

Luke–Acts (Laura Pasterkamp).[6] In both projects, a double heuristic is at work. First, the question is asked as to where the presence of children may be surmised, which has, amongst other things, to do with the historical imagination of protagonists and groups of protagonists (e.g., how old are people imagined to be and what composition of groups is assumed implicitly or explicitly). This can already lead to a substantial revision of how early Christian communities are imagined (given that they are usually imagined as groups of adults, which is, in fact, quite questionable on historical grounds). Second, it is asked what the experience of children in the past (and, to a certain extent, in the present) may have been in relation to events referred to in texts. This goes beyond working out where one might have to think that children were present and seeks to highlight what may have been their experience of the early Christian movement, which adds considerably to the historical imagination of the same. One step further is to also include the perspectives of contemporary children on ancient texts, which, as experience shows, leads to perspectives that can be surprising and enriching in equal measure.[7]

In the current volume, the original Dom Hélder Câmara Lecture of Shantelle Weber takes centre stage. Entitled "Jesus loves me this I know, DOES the Bible tell me so?," it takes as its point of departure a well-known children's song and investigates what it would mean if the experience of children, and with that, a childist perspective, is placed at the heart of being a church and of biblical interpretation. The world of children is diverse and often beautiful, yet just as frequently it can be marred by experiences of brokenness and violence. Biblical perspectives on children are subsequently explored, embracing a contextual biblical approach, in order to centre children in the reading of biblical texts. The paper asks the critical question as to what needs to be changed and reconceptualized in received theological convictions when revisiting them from a childist perspective.

Weber's paper is followed by one that emerged out of the original responses to the lecture by Corina Nagel-Herweijer and Ronelle Sonnenberg and has now become a joint paper. In "Seeing and experiencing things differently. How the theologizing of children can contribute to theology," the authors provide a conceptual clarification of what is meant with terms such as "child theology" and "children's theology" in order to find a position from which to ask the question as to how children's theology can contribute to theology at

6 See already: Pasterkamp, "Een jong meisje."

7 See, for instance the overview offered in: Betsworth and Parker, eds., *T&T Clark Handbook*; see from a Dutch context also: Smit, Veerbeek and Nagel, "Hoe jongeren."

large. In doing so, both the social constructivism on which the paradigm of children's theology is based is addressed and a proposal is made to include God explicitly as an actor in such forms of theology. Furthermore, the paper argues that children can offer perspectives that (adult) professional theologians cannot offer (any longer), which is substantiated with reference to a set of case studies.

The third paper included in this volume is entitled "Child theology, spirituality and intersectionality." Authored by Annemie Dillen and Amy Casteel, the paper uses the discourse on the "oppression Olympics" in which various kinds of experiences of being oppressed as a child compete. Drawing on Mark 10:13–16 (and especially on v. 15), the authors argue that such a competition is to be avoided by considering the intersectional experience of oppression that a child may have. At the same time, there should also be an openness to the fact that not every issue can be resolved at the same time, or is even within the grasp of human beings to begin with, if a struggle for justice, particularly for children, remains necessary. The paper thus both rereads a biblical text and proceeds to use it as a building block for a childist perspective in theology.

In Armin Kummer's "What Hope for Children? Eschatology, the Normativity of the Future, and Christian Hope in Godly Play," the "Godly Play" method for introducing children to the faith and the church's liturgy is the focus of attention. This method aims to instill a "playful orthodoxy" and has become very popular in a variety of churches, in several translations and adaptations. In particular, it asks what role the notion of hope (and with that: eschatology) plays in this method. Finding the method lacking, an argument is made for enriching it in this respect by engaging with and integrating insights from the "Normativity of the Future" approach to biblical hermeneutics, as it has been developed by Reimund Bieringer.

Focusing on the context of the Philippines, Justin Joseph G. Badion and Julius Anthony L. Porqueriño's "'Unbinding' Children's Roles in Philippine Catholic Religious Education" investigates the role of children in Philippine Catholic schools, focusing in particular on the use of the story of the binding of Isaac (Gen. 22:1–19). Critiquing, on the one hand, the silencing of children in traditional educational practices, the authors also interpret the story of their choice with the aid of insights from contextual hermeneutics and child theology, thereby arriving at a pedagogical proposal regarding the binding of Isaac that encourages children's active participation and critical thinking. In doing so, this study argues for a paradigm shift in religious education to align itself much more with the concerns highlighted in child theology and childist hermeneutics.

In the final thematic paper, Erik Renkema shifts the focus to teachers and what might be expected from them when it comes to pedagogically negotiating religion, worldview and diversity in a school context ("Religion, Worldview and Diversity in School: What to Expect from Teachers?"). As the religious questions and experiences of children are a key dimension in the development of a personal identity of children, and as dialogue is key to negotiating differences in the classroom when it comes to religion and worldview, a teacher should have particular hermeneutical and communication skills. In particular, the author proposes that a teacher should be able to fulfil the roles of translation, imaginator, moderator, explorer, and source, in order to facilitate children's engagement in child theology in a dialogical fashion.

The final full paper included in this volume is authored by one of the leading scholars in the field of Contextual Biblical Interpretation: Gerald West. Drawing on his vast experience in the field in his paper "CBI as a (Biblical Studies) Discipline," West makes a proposal for identifying key conceptual parameters that determine family of forms of Contextual Biblical Interpretation (the context functions as the subject of interpretation; the context is a "real life" one; the interpretation has a commitment to social and theological transformation; interpretations both make use of and challenge the resources of biblical studies; interpretations contribute to changing the field of biblical studies). Working through these conceptual parameters systematically, West both illustrates and substantiates his proposal and offers a map of the field at the same time.

Rounding off this volume is a set of reviews of pertinent literature: Sharon Betsworth and Julie Faith Parker's *T&T Clark Handbook of Children in the Bible and the Biblical World* is reviewed by Laura Pasterkamp; and Klaas Spronk reviews Margaret Murray Talbot's *Why Jephthah's Daughter Weeps: A Child-Oriented Interpretation.*

The research presented in this volume is representative of the kind of research that the Centre for Contextual Biblical Interpretation seeks to further and make available. It promotes it for heuristic and hermeneutical reasons and because of the ethical conviction that unheard, or even silenced, voices are worth listening to. In doing so, an organic relationship between scholarly research and social (and ecclesial) matters also emerges, for instance the issues encapsulated by the UN's Sustainable Development Goals, which can be reflected upon in dialogue with the ancient texts concerned. As we believe that this is a valuable enterprise, we are grateful to Amsterdam University Press for the good cooperation, to the esteemed members of the editorial board who are giving their time, talent and good name to the YBCI, to our institutions for supporting our scholarly endeavours in general, and to the various partners that support this endeavour: the Arminius Institute, the Amsterdam Sustainability Institute, Kerk in Actie, the Vrijzinnige Fondsen, CLUE+, the University Library (including its Open Access Fund) and the Faculty of Religion and Theology (Vrije Universiteit Amsterdam), and the Protestant Theological University.

Last, but certainly not least, particular thanks go not just to the contributors to this volume, but also to Pieter Dirk Dekker for his work in starting up the YBCI and to Ronald de Jong for making it work!

Bibliography

Alkhouri, Yousef Kamal. "The Kingdom of God and Empires. A Contemporary Palestinian Christian Contextual Biblical Interpretation." PhD dissertation, Vrije Universiteit Amsterdam, 2024.

Betsworth, Sharon and Julie Faith Parker, eds. *T&T Clark Handbook of Children in the Bible and the Biblical World*. London: T&T Clark, 2019.

Furlong, Dean. "The Identification of John the Evangelist in the Early Church." PhD dissertation, Vrije Universiteit Amsterdam, 2017.

Ham, Kirsten van der, and Catharina Margaretha van Vliet. "Experiencing Ecumenism in an International Theological Exchange Programme: Bridging the Gap Between Grassroots Ecumenism and the Ecumenical Movement." *International Review of Mission* 109 (2020): 340–53.

Ham, Kirsten van der, Geke van Vliet, Klaas Spronk, and Peter-Ben Smit, eds. *Building Bridges Towards a More Humane Society. Explorations in Contextual Biblical Interpretation on the Occasion of the 25th Anniversary of the Bridging Gaps Exchange Program*. Geneva: Globethics, 2022.

Ham, Kirsten van der, Nienke Pruiksma, Geke van Vliet, and Peter-Ben Smit, eds. *Opstandig leven. Bijbelse en theologische perspectieven op goed leven*. Utrecht: NZR, 2022.

Holmgaard, Christian. "On Earth as it is in Heaven. New Creation in Matthew's Gospel." PhD dissertation, Vrije Universiteit Amsterdam, 2018.

King, Zachary. "The Motifs of Growth, Absent Master and Wedding Feast in the Parables. An Early Christian Argument for the Delay of the Parousia as Impetus for Gentile Inclusion." PhD dissertation, Vrije Universiteit Amsterdam, 2017.

Lawrence, Louise, Hannah Strømmen, Peter-Ben Smit, and Charlene van der Walt, eds. *Challenging Contextuality: Bibles and Biblical Scholarship in Context*. Oxford: Oxford University Press, 2024.

Moreno Palacios, Pablo. "Impacto del neopentecostalismo en la identidad de los bautistas de Cali, Colombia." PhD dissertation, Vrije Universiteit Amsterdam, 2024.

Noort, Gerrit, Astrid Hamberg, Mart-Jan Luteyn, Kirsten van der Ham, and Peter-Ben Smit, eds. *Bijbel en 'beperking'. Contextuele en Missiologische Perspectieven.* Driebergen: NZR, 2019.

Pasterkamp, Laura. "Een jong meisje het zwijgen opgelegd?" *Kerk en Theologie* 74 (2023): 380–98.

Pruiksma, Nienke, Kirsten van der Ham, Mart Jan Luteyn, Geke van Vliet, and Peter-Ben Smit, eds. *De schepping in het midden. Klimaatcrisis als theologische uitdaging.* Driebergen: NZR, 2020.

Punt, Jeremy. "Armoede, Gender, Seks, en De Bijbel." *Kerk en Theologie* 75 (2024): 261–86.

Sarot, Marcel, and Peter-Ben Smit, eds. *De toekomst van de oecumene in Europa*, Perspectief 2023-61. Accessed on October 7, 2024. https://www.oecumene.nl/perspectief/2024/04/perspectief-2023-61/.

Schipani, Daniel, Martien E. Brinkman, and Hans Snoek, eds. *New Perspectives on Intercultural Reading of the Bible: Hermeneutical Explorations in Honor of Hans de Wit.* Elkhart: Institute of Mennonite Studies, 2015.

Smit, Peter-Ben. "Contextuele bijbelinterpretatie bestaat niet, en dat is maar goed ook." In *De Bijbel in Nederland. Reflecties over het gebruik van de Bijbel in kerk en cultuur*, edited by Sake Stoppels, Floor Barnhoorn and Anne-Mareike Schol-Wette. Haarlem: Nederlands Bijbelgenootschap, 2018, 72–85.

Smit, Peter-Ben, Iris Veerbeek, and Corina Nagel. "Hoe jongeren vanuit hun context de Bijbel lezen." *Tijdschrift voor geestelijk leven* 77.2 (2021): 35–45.

Snoek, Hans, ed. *In Love with the Bible and its Ordinary Readers. Hans De Wit and the Intercultural Bible Reading Project.* Elkhart: Institute of Mennonite Studies, 2015.

Spronk, Klaas, Joep Dubbink, and Peter-Ben Smit, eds. *Bijbel en context in Nederland.* Thematic issue of *Kerk en theologie* 72:2 [2021].

Spronk, Klaas, Kirsten van der Ham, and Peter-Ben Smit. "Contextual Biblical Intepretation: A Theological Necessity." *Concilium* 2022:3 (2022): 15–24.

Troost, Ari C. "Exegetical Bodybuilding Gender and Interpretation in Luke 1–2." PhD dissertation, Utrecht University, 2019.

Visser, Jacoba Maryna Helena. "Perfecting Poverty. A Rhetorical Investigation of Poverty and Masculinities Intersecting in James." PhD dissertation, Vrije Universiteit Amsterdam, 2021.

Washam, Jamie. "Regenerating the Garden of the World." PhD dissertation, Vrije Universiteit Amsterdam, 2022.

Wit, Hans de, and Janet Dyk, eds. *Bible and Transformation. The Promise of Intercultural Bible Reading.* Atlanta: SBL, 2015.

Wit, Hans de, Marleen Kool, and Daniel Schipani, eds. *Through the Eyes of Another. Intercultural Reading of the Bible.* Elkhart: Institute of Mennonite Studies, 2004.

Amsterdam University Press

YEARBOOK OF CONTEXTUAL BIBLICAL INTERPRETATION 1 (2024) 8-26
HTTPS://DOI.ORG/10.5117/YCBI2024.002.WEBE

Jesus loves me this I know, DOES the Bible tell me so?

Shantelle Weber, Faculty of Theology, University of Stellenbosch, smweber@sun.ac.za

Abstract

The children's song "Jesus Loves Me" originated in the nineteenth century. Over the years, "Jesus Loves Me" has become a popular Christian hymn and a well-loved song in Sunday schools, churches, and Christian households around the world. Children are part of families, schools, local and faith communities. Their arrival as infants is welcomed in most cultures and environments across the world. The reality of a fallen and broken world is that many children live and grow into communities which are not safe, welcoming, or capable of nurturing these. This paper reflects on this children's ministry song's simple, yet powerful lyrics aimed at conveying the message of Jesus' love in a way that is easy for children to understand and remember. Through the lens of a somewhat liberal theology and reflecting on the complexity of the marginalized/vulnerable child, I would like to explore what the reality of Jesus' love in a fallen and broken world looks like when the child is indeed placed at the center of how we are church. Through the lens of the discipline of Child Theology, I further explore what the Bible does say about the child in our midst. Teaching the faith is probably our most difficult task. What children need more than anything else is living faith in Christ. Parents, teachers, and Christian leaders must devote all of their energy and enthusiasm to presenting Christ to their children.

Keywords: Children, Child Theology, Contextual Bible study, violence, faith community.

Introduction

Jesus loves me—this I know,
For the Bible tells me so:
Little ones to him belong, —
They are weak, but he is strong.

Jesus loves me—he who died
Heaven's gate to open wide;
He will wash away my sin,
Let his little child come in.

The children's song "Jesus Loves Me" originated in the nineteenth century. It is believed to have been written by Anna B. Warner in 1860, with music composed by William B. Bradbury. Over the years, "Jesus Loves Me" has become a popular Christian hymn and a well-loved song in Sunday schools, churches, and Christian households around the world. Two significant things about this song have been its simplicity in words and melody, and its reminder of God's love and faith for all ages.

Children are part of families, schools, local and faith communities. Their arrival as infants is welcomed in most cultures and environments across the world. This is celebrated through varying socio-cultural (initiation rites of passage, naming ceremonies, etc.) and religious celebrations (prayers of dedication, baptism, etc). Within faith communities, we are accustomed to the call for children to be the future of the church. Verses like Ps. 127:3 celebrating children as a blessing or inheritance from God are used to express their place and significance in our families and churches. Scriptural texts like these have been highlighted to agree that children are given to us by God.

The reality of a fallen and broken world is that many children live and grow into communities which are not safe, welcoming, or capable of nurturing these. Increasing and complex pressures on primary caregivers, guardians, and families affect children. Children are grounded within culture, history, communities, families, relationships, and systems. If these contextual realities are ignored, the wider circumstances which contribute to the adversity that some children experience will not be effectively addressed.[1] According to Grobbelaar, children are the most marginalized group in all of history.[2] He adds, however, that the child population group is not

1 Ansell, *Children*, 28.

2 Grobbelaar and Jones, eds., *Childhood vulnerabilities*, 15.

a homogeneous group of people living in the same situations. They are a diverse group of people living in diverse contexts with different real-life experiences.[3] When reflecting on this notion of marginalization we should also consider Grobbelaar's discussion on vulnerability.[4] He says that when we start to think and talk about vulnerable as "them", "as different from us" and as emphasizing the child's "otherness" and only seeing them as subjects of our benevolence, we view them through strong paternalistic attitudes and agendas. Through such approaches, we (the adults, the powerful) decide who are vulnerable, what their vulnerability is and what exactly they need as victims. What is clear through much research on children is that their vulnerabilities are not of their own doing and therefore they have legitimate claims to protection and resources. Reflecting on Collins, he encourages us to start thinking about the child's vulnerability as a real-life concept in which the lived experience of the child is placed at the center of our reflections of such vulnerability:[5]

> Whilst children in many of these diverse contexts have positive experiences of belonging and of having their human dignity respected, there are even more who are practically invisible and excluded, whose voices are ignored, and whose needs are not attended to.[6]

Koopman agrees that it is when children's basic needs for a dignified life are not met that they become vulnerable.[7] This reality is elaborated later in this paper.

Many Christian faith communities hold the Bible as integral text of and for their faith. Many creeds and ecclesial constitutions or policies place the Bible as one of the ways God communicates to us. Surely it is our hope and expectation in making the Bible both available and accessible to the youngest ones in our midst; that in hearing stories of God's people a long time ago, in reading poetry and in seeing the people that Jesus welcomed, we learn together what it means to live in this world.[8] Many evangelical communities teach children Bible memory verses from a young age in the hope that this word of God would remain a crucial part of the child's faith journey. Protestant evangelical and conservative churches have been more

3 Grobbelaar and Jones eds., *Childhood vulnerabilities*, 3.
4 Grobbelaar and Jones eds., *Childhood vulnerabilities*, 5–15.
5 Collins, "The contours of 'vulnerability,'" 64.
6 De Boeck and Honwana, "Children and youth in Africa," 1–2.
7 Grobbelaar and Breed. eds., *Theologies*, 193–209.
8 Caldwell, "Reading the Bible with Children," 457.

vocal in nationwide debates about familial issues and have established practical programs to address the needs of children and their families. However, many churches do not always adequately address the spiritual questions of children themselves, what children might teach adults, and the responsibilities of parents, the church, and the state to protect and support children.[9] The sad reality seems to be that the *assumed* value placed on our children and on the place of the biblical text in our faith, does not seem to translate into how we view children today. Hence my play on the term: "does the Bible really tell us so".

Reflecting on the traditional position and role of the Bible through the lens of a child's vulnerability, we realise that we have thought about the marginalization and vulnerability of the child through deficit lenses. Our theological approaches to children have reflected dominant developmental ideas which imagine children as in some way incomplete, not fully developed and dependent on adults.[10] I agree that an almost universal concept of childhood as a life stage that is different from adulthood prevails, but I am arguing that how we define what this difference or differences are leads to different conceptions of childhood.[11] Thus, our conceptions of childhood are contextually bound and are influenced by social, economic, historic, and political circumstances and changes over time. This includes ecclesial teachings and cultures concerning the child. A deficit and most likely one-sided approach to children becomes very disempowering, giving minimal space for their agency and participation as equal human beings with adults, over-emphasizing their protection rights and leaning towards the patronizing. This means we need to be careful of assuming that as the marginalized voice, as the vulnerable voice, we label these children and with our labels we stereotype these children because it is not only our thoughts about them that are influenced in this way but also our attitudes and actions towards them, their situations and other role players in their contexts.[12]

Against the above-mentioned background, this paper reflects on this children's ministry song's simple, yet powerful lyrics aimed at conveying the message of Jesus' love in a way that is easy for children to understand and remember. Through the lens of a somewhat liberal theology and reflecting on the complexity of the marginalized/vulnerable child, I would like to explore what the reality of Jesus' love in a fallen and broken world looks

9 Bunge, *Child*, 12.

10 Grobbelaar and Jones, eds., *Theologies*, 11.

11 Grobbelaar and Jones, eds., *Theologies*, 12.

12 Grobbelaar and Jones, eds., *Theologies*, 15.

like when the child is indeed placed at the centre of how we are church. Through the lens of the discipline of Child Theology, I would like to further explore what the Bible does say about the child in our midst.

Love: Importance of the Child in Our Midst

Biblical scholar Musa Dube argues that it is important to establish a biblical basis for making children feel welcome in church and society. For her this essentially implies that wherever children feel uncomfortable and wherever their rights and needs are not met, including in the church, it means that "not only [are] they unwelcome, but God is not welcomed."[13] At this point I note the difference between children's ministry which takes the biblical imperative to care for and nurture of the faith of our children seriously and child theology, which intentionally reflects on the place and role of the child in the Bible. Reminded of the paternalistic approach to the child, various scholars have focussed on the former which is exclusively based on the way adults could deal with children without acknowledging the ways in which children as social agents could themselves contribute.

I have already mentioned that children cannot be viewed as a homogeneous group. Some children experience First World access to education, health care and public utilities, while others succumb to hunger, ill-health, neglect, violence, and death.[14] Perhaps the call is to reflect on your own context for a moment. Think about any instance when a child walked into the company. How did this child/ren's presence affect the space? Were we distracted from our initial conversation or activity? Was the volume and language in which we spoke altered because of the child? For the purposes of our current discussion, let's reflect together on what the presence of a vulnerable/marginalised child looks like? I opt in this paper for reflection on one aspect of such vulnerability: child violence. Think again with me, about your context, now specifically reflecting on how children are portrayed in the media. I always wonder what the purpose of showing photos of vulnerable children on television or media calls for funding is? Does seeing the child influence our concern for the hungry, malnourished, or homeless child make it easier to address the need? Maybe travelling to the country where these children are better sensitizes us to their need? Marginalized or centred,

13 Dube, "Fighting with God," 32.

14 De Beer and James, "Recovering a gospel," 78.

what does our theology of God's unconditional love calls us toward? The presence of any children in our midst cannot be ignored.

The UN Convention on the rights of the child promotes, at its core, freedom from any violation that compromises a child's rights or hinders their social progress.[15] The 2019 JLI Ending violence against children learning hub report[16] discusses violence against children in diverse contexts noting violence as a global problem that affects children of all ages, genders, and backgrounds. The report highlights that violence against children is often hidden, underreported, and normalized in many cultures and communities. It highlights online or cyber violence, child to child abuse against children and narratives of witchcraft related to children as the three core forms of violence.[17] The internet has fuelled a new form of abuse against children through the rise in child pornography and the use of social media by sexual predators and cyberbullies targeting children. Trusted individuals within religious institutions are mentioned as exploiting social media and the internet to access children for harmful purposes. Child-to-child abuse includes instances of physical, emotional, and sexual violence occurring between peers, older and younger children, and both boys and girls. Group bullying is also mentioned as a form of child-to-child abuse.

Palm argues that when we consider such violence towards and among our children, we need to ask how this relates to our faith.[18] She argues that ancient sacred texts take patriarchy (for example the rule of the fathers) for granted. As a result, literal readings of these texts today can be highly damaging for children. We see this in the entrenched social norms that perpetuate hierarchical ways of viewing children as patriarchal property. Punt confirms that studies of children's lives in ancient times suffer from a deficit of material available directly from children and often rely on evidence from adults, usually elite men.[19] As noted earlier, this places adults in a superior position over children and makes vulnerable children more voiceless and invisible. Palm further notes that religious belief systems often shape what many adults believe is best for their children because of their belief of what God's will is.[20] The challenge is that these beliefs often become entangled with cultural norms created within faith communities and must be tackled directly by faith leaders. I dare call us to consider what spiritual neglect or

15 Palm, *Scoping*.
16 Palm, *Scoping*, 9, 12, 31.
17 Palm, *Scoping*, 14.
18 Palm, *Scoping*, 56–8.
19 Punt, "Children's Lives," 63.
20 Palm, *Scoping*.

forms of violence could have crept into our lack of taking the lived realities of children and their faith formation seriously. So, the question I have is how do we express or embody God's love as church, as family, as faith leaders in a such a violent and contradictory world, a world that is not separated from us as the church? Does Jesus truly love every child and how do we as his church exemplify this love as we live and experience such children every day?

Reflection on the Bible for/with Children in Our Midst

Childhood has not always been a marginal theme in theology. Prior to the mid-nineteenth century, theologians reflected on issues of child rearing, education, moral and spiritual formation. Several theologians wrote catechisms and were directly involved with the education of children. Luther and Calvin wrote catechisms for use in the home and encouraged parents, especially fathers, to take responsibility for the moral and spiritual formation of their children. Bushnell and Schleiermacher[21] considered teaching children a crucial aspect of their ministry and theological reflection. This is generally not the case among most twentieth-century theologians. The absence of well-developed and historically and biblically informed teachings about children explain why many churches often struggle to create and to sustain strong programs in religious education and in child-advocacy ministry. Child Theology differs from traditional theological approaches in that it places the child or children at the centre of theological reflection. It is a way of studying the Bible and doing theology that takes as its starting point the example of Jesus when He placed a little child amid the disciples.

The child is commonly seen in the New Testament either amid the crowds which followed or encountered Jesus on the street or in the context of their families. Children take their place alongside adults in the community of disciples. Let's reflect on the metaphoric example from Matt. 18:2–5 (New Living Translation):

> 2 Jesus called a little child to him and put the child among them. 3 Then he said, "I tell you the truth, unless you turn from your sins and become like little children, you will never get into the Kingdom of Heaven. 4 So anyone who becomes as humble as this little child is the greatest in the Kingdom of Heaven. 5 And anyone who welcomes a little child like this on my behalf is welcoming me.

21 Bunge, *Child*, 11.

The socio-cultural context of this text is first century Mediterranean world. The difference in Hellenistic and Judaic cultures is prevalent. It is an androcentric culture in which men are considered superior to women and the family structure was essentially patriarchal. Children were viewed as property belonging to the father, who played the primary role in the education of children.

> Children's lives and activities were framed also by the agonistic nature of first-century society, making them susceptible to structural violence in various ways [...] Even the lives of children of the elite were not spared if political interests came in the way.[22]

Ninety percent of the population were peasants who struggled financially, resulting in more than seventy percent of the population living below the breadline. This meant that as early as the age of five, boys had to gather the harvest, and girls had to begin baking bread. Poor economic structures affected hygienic conditions resulting in children getting ill from malnutrition. Child death toll was generally very high amongst children with infant mortality rates sometimes reaching thirty percent. It is clear in this context that childhood was seen as an incomplete state of being that was a mere prelude for adulthood. Children's value laid primarily in their future contributions as adults. Despite societal and adult views on children, this text reveals that Jesus identifies with a child and equates welcoming a little child in his name to welcoming himself and the One who sent him. He depicts children as models for adults of entering the reign of God, as models of greatness and vehicles of divine revelation. Jesus did not treat children according to the position of children under the Jewish religious law of his time. The text also assumes that there is special place in Jesus' heart for all "the downtrodden and despised of the world," of which children were a part.[23]

From a literal hermeneutical perspective,[24] several other biblical texts reflect Christ receiving children, blessing them, touching them, and healing them, indignant toward those who have contempt for them.[25] We learn about children like the daughter of Jairus (Matt. 9:18–26); the daughter of the Canaanite woman (Matt. 15:21–28) and a boy with a demon (Matt.

22 Punt, "Children's lives," 60–1.

23 Bunge, *Child*, 11.

24 The author of this chapter is not a biblical scholar and writes from a practical theological perspective in which the contextual realities of the child is prioritised in a larger biblical narrative.

25 Matt. 11:25; 18:1–5; 19:13–15; 21:14–16; Mark 9:33–37; 10:13–16; Luke 9:46–48; 18:15–17.

17:14–20) all being healed by him. This all took place in the paternalistic world where men usually had little contact with children and especially did not reach out to girls, Jesus acted quite differently in these miracles.

Barnett notes that in 1 Cor. 13, Paul places the metaphoric image of the child amid the divided and competing community of Corinth to remind them of the importance of relationships over status.[26] Perhaps his action reminds us a bit of Jesus, placing the child amongst the disciples arguing over who is the greatest. The gift of the child in 1 Cor. 13 is that it provides a positive model for us. Here, the child represents vulnerability, universality, and non-utilitarianism, and provides an inclusive relational ethic of love. She argues that the paradigm of child as the vulnerable relational agent in our midst does not replace the crucified Christ as the paradigm of grace but gives a concrete and contingent model from which we might practice a "more excellent way". Reflecting on using children as models of faith, Schleiermacher's and Rahner's[27] theological positions led them to regard children both as human being worthy of respect and dignity and as models for adults. Rahner asserts that children have value and dignity and are fully human from the beginning. Respect them and have reverence for them from the start. They are examples because they lack false ambition and artificiality.

Child Theology answers the need for theological reflection about children if we are serious about creating ecologies of faith formation where family practices overlap with church practices and different generations are given the opportunity to worship together, serve together and pray together during worship services and at home.[28] Theological reflection and consideration about children are needed to impact an 'operational theology' that treats children as consumers and involves them in worship services only as ornaments or tokens for special days and festivals.

Child Theology is akin to other new theologies that have brought new questions to the Bible. These questions are based on the experiences of those who had long been marginal to formal theological reflection: the poor, the women, the marginalised races that have brought to us liberation, feminine and black theologies.[29] This "new" field might assist us not only in thinking about how faith formation does and should take place ("operative theology"), but how we consider the most oppressed social group, comprising

26 Barnett, *Children*.
27 Bunge, *Child*, 18.
28 Matthaei, "Rethinking faith formation."
29 Collier, *Toddling*, 8.

half of the world's population, when we think about "what is meant by 'the kingdom of God' and how we are to live in God's way."[30] Grobbelaar uses a beautiful quote by Denise Ackermann (from her book: "After the Locusts: Letters from a Landscape of Faith") when describing the nature of theology: "Theology is worrying about what God is worrying about when God gets up in the morning."[31] In the case of Child Theology, it is specifically doing theology in a way that helps us understand and become sensitive for the way God worries about the children of this world. Child Theology concerns itself with the way God cries about the brokenness of children, how God gets angry at those who cause them pain and God's joy when they are welcomed and healed.[32]

Listening to the Voice of Children in Theology and Bible Interpretation

According to De Beer and James, children have served as the primary catalysts of conversion. Children have always, and continue, to call the church to a new conversion, from institutional building, the development of empire and the indulging of the middle class to the reversal of human hierarchies of status and power and to establishing the reign of God, which is a reign of love and justice.[33] In 2012, Swart and Yates highlighted from empirical research, that

> children and their well-being constitute a marginal theme in practical theological interpretation in the context of the academy; the normative basis that should guide practical theologians' views of children is lacking, asking the important question of whether it should not be the task and responsibility of every theologian, on the basis of the Christian faith, to include children in particular moments of practical theological interpretation.[34]

According to Swart and Yates,[35] listening to children in the process of practical theological interpretation will offer newly found opportunities

30 Bunge, *Child*, 9.
31 Grobbelaar, *Child*, 7–19.
32 Grobbelaar, *Child*, 9.
33 Prevette, White, Ewell, and Konz, *Theology*, 88.
34 Swart and Yates, *Listening*, 9–10.
35 Swart and Yates, *Listening*, 1.

for Christian theology and the church to contribute to the well-being of children as a local, national, continental, and global public concern. Listening to children's voices does not only address questions about social justice and the participation rights of children and children's position as active agents in society. The act of listening to children is also about the survival and development of children, caring for them and protecting them from living conditions that dehumanise them—a way of promoting the human dignity of children as the image of God in each human being. It is also about communicating and being in relationship with children to realise supportive and companionable interactions in adult-child spaces. When adults listen to children, they therefore do not only make it their responsibility to remain in touch with the well-being of children as this is experienced by children themselves, but they also take responsibility for the responsibility of children to listen to and treat others respectfully.[36]

This paper was initially presented as the 2023 annual Dom Helder Camara lecture under the auspices of the Centre for contextual biblical interpretation at the Vrije and PThU Universities. From my very brief understanding of the Archbishop of Olinde and Recife in Northeastern Brazil, he seems to have been quite a radical leader and poet, passionate about the justice and peace of humanity. It seems he had a commitment to non-violence as a means of revolutionary change.

> When children are abused, neglected and discriminated against in society, the academy and the church therefore have to co-construct ministries of advocacy, care, teaching, preaching and service to be acting in the best interests of those children and their right to social justice.[37]

What many are not aware of (or at least I was not), is that the lyrics of the song "Jesus loves me" first appeared as a poem in the context of an 1860 novel called Say and Seal, written by Anna's older sister Susan Warner, in which the words were spoken as a comforting poem to a dying child. The novel is a Christian fiction work that focuses on the themes of faith, family, and moral values. It tells the story of a young girl named Faith Derrick and her experiences as she grows up in a religious and close-knit community. The novel explores the challenges and trials she faces and how her faith plays a significant role in helping her navigate life's obstacles. It teaches us about the importance of faith, family, and community support, moral values,

36 Dillen, "Children between liberation and care," 245.

37 Swart and Yates, *Listening*, 2.

forgiveness, resilience, love, and the role of religion in shaping our lives. I highlight this to stress the importance of taking the context of the child and the context of the sources we use in engaging these children seriously.

Contextual Bible Study (CBS) has developed as an intercultural biblical hermeneutic within a particular form of liberation hermeneutics that emerged in the 1980s.[38] Context is an integral part of the interpretive process but not all contexts are given the same epistemological privilege in liberation hermeneutics. CBS is

> dialogical, including not only the dialogue between context and the biblical text but also a dialogue between "ordinary" and "scholarly" readers as they together, in some way, dialogue with the Bible. It is a collaborative and communal process.[39]

Hans de Wit calls for the importance of exegesis for spontaneous understanding of the text.[40] He goes on to examine what can and does happen "when ordinary and professional readers sit across from each other," but without making it clear how the presence of each and their respective resources is constitutive of the reading process. Nevertheless, there is a clear recognition that ordinary (and perhaps childlike) readings offer a "gift" to the exegete and can "orient" the exegete in her or his scholarly work.[41] Reflecting on the work of CBS, Gerald West notes his concern that liberation hermeneutics as a method that advocates for the epistemological privilege of the poor, has been so reluctant to acknowledge the contribution of the poor to the process of understanding the biblical text.[42] In response to this, an intercultural biblical hermeneutics adds its voice to those of us who insist on the "exegetical" contribution of the poor. Too often, these insights have unfortunately been done without considering the voices and agency of children. "It is as alarming as doing black theology in spaces where no black voices participate, or liberation theology without the physical presence and offensiveness of the poor."[43]

Here, I make the connection to what I experience a marginalization of children in theological reflection and within ecclesial spaces. The Bible has in several ways and contexts spoken into the lives of the child, yet the church

38 West, 'Locating "Contextual Bible Study"', 1.
39 De Andrade, Segovia, and Tolbert, *Reading*.
40 De Wit, Jonker, Kool, and Schipani, *Through the eyes*, 71.
41 De Wit, Jonker, Kool, and Schipani, *Through the eyes*, 78.
42 West, "Locating 'Contextual Bible Study,'" 5.
43 Weber and De Beer, "Doing theology," 2.

and academy have not prioritised teaching and learning from the child in this regard. The 1910 Edinburgh Missionary Conference highlighted the need for each generation to hear the gospel afresh in its own time resulting in the work of the "4/14 Window" which is aimed at focusing on the need to engage missionally with children aged roughly between 4 and 14 years old. Children cannot be regarded as "future church" or as some sort of appendage to Christian adults. They should be given full rights to both hear and embrace the gospel on their own terms and to become witnesses themselves to the transforming power of God in Christ Jesus.[44] In 2000, the Micah Network for Integral Mission called for "holistic Child Development" as a way of working with children to enable them to develop every aspect to their humanity and to contribute at each stage of their development to the community of which they are a part.[45] If we deny children a place in mission (as in the church), we will distort the image of God we are called to reflect in our world. To engage in mission as the body of Christ without the child is to walk with one leg or to see with one eye. It seems that our lens of the child as the future of the church has crippled our effectiveness in a world where children are the majority population, daily intersecting with complex lived realities that could inform how we read the text and teach this text.

CBS works overtly with a contested Bible,[46] drawing on the full array of socio-historical[47]or literary[48] or symbolic-metaphorical[49] resources to discern the contending voices of particular texts, privileging marginalised voices. However, for some, the voices of the marginalised within the text are so compromised by layers of dominating discourse that the Bible can only be an instrumentalist resource, not a substantive resource.[50] Nonetheless, some of these continue to use the Bible because they recognise that the masses of ordinary readers consider it a sacred and substantive "silo or storeroom."[51] Palm reminds us through the work of Janet Pais (1971) that the need for a liberation theology for the child is not new:

44 Oxbrow, "Christian mission," 53–4.
45 Oxbrow, "Christian mission," 53–4.
46 Anderson, *Ancient*, 1.
47 Mosala and Horsley, *A materialist reading.*
48 Trible, "Depatriarchalization in biblical interpretation."
49 Schneiders, "Feminist ideology."
50 West, "And the Dumb," 103–30.
51 Mofokeng, "Black Christians," 40.

> As early as the 1970s Pais identified children as an oppressed group who are inherently disadvantaged due to their lack of access to power or resources that is equal to the adults around them and because they can also be socialized into normalizing the violence around them.[52]

She (Palm) also refers to Craig Nessan's work which says child liberation theology takes seriously the research and social analysis that conclusively demonstrates the serious and lasting harm done to children through oppression.[53] She further calls on the work of Ryan Stollar who points out that ignoring children suffering is often shaped by a philosophy of "adultism" where faith beliefs are seen from an adult perspective rather than paying attention to whether they are liberating for children.[54] Palm further urges us as a church and as Christians to find ways to reimagine God as a child in order to speak about God from the lived experience of suffering children.[55] This requires refusing to read faith traditions and texts through the eyes of adults only but paying close attention to how they are seen from a child's perspective.

In a research study titled "Dutch children and their 'God,'" Ter Avest differentiated between the understanding of God among indigenous and immigrant children by examining the development of the "God" concept among pupils at two primary schools.[56] The study also explored the differences in interpretation of stories from different religious traditions among indigenous and immigrant children. It found that indigenous pupils tended to explore new possible interpretations more than children with a migrant and Islamic background, and girls more than boys. Several factors influenced how children understand God, including their socialization process at home, their religious sensitivity, and their competency for inter-religious dialogue. The place of the child in contextual hermeneutics is a central focus of Child Theology. Child Theology is a way of studying the Bible and doing theology that takes as its starting point the example of Jesus when he placed a little child amid the disciples.

Reflecting on the African context, the African concept of "child" is closely tied with the concept of self and community, and there can be no keener revelation of a society's soul than the way they treat their children. Child

52 Palm, *Scoping*.
53 Nessan, "Child Liberation Theology."
54 Stoller, *Towards*.
55 Palm, *Scoping*, 58–60.
56 Avest, "Dutch children."

Theology is an attempt to respond to the question of whether we can read and interpret the Bible in Africa (and most likely elsewhere) from the Child Theology vantage point.[57] Firstly, it is that most children in Africa are facing abuses of unprecedented proportions. Secondly, "child" as part of family (reality and metaphor) is also a hermeneutical tool to read, interpret, and analyse the biblical text in Africa by using the family as a hermeneutical procedure, paradigm, and methodology through which the Bible could be read and interpreted. The family is viewed as a reality and a metaphor, and the study of the family is once again gaining momentum among biblical scholars.

> At the center of Christian faith, is the confession that God experienced human life, including the early terrors of a refugee childhood at risk of violent death. This God then not only welcomes children but makes the child a sacrament of the kin-dom or community of God and insists that it is only when adults honour and respect children and identify with the child in themselves that they know how to participate in kin-dom existence. The theme of a pilgrim child is used to view children as offering unique gifts to adults which must be respected in all their graced vulnerability.[58]

Reflecting on the original poem written by Susan Warner through the lens of the child, we take the child in our midst and in the Bible seriously, because we believe that the way that children are educated in the Christian faith will have profound consequences on their future lives, both as individuals and as members of the Christian church. Children will take in the language of Christian faith in the same way that they learn their mother tongue. When children who have been raised in the church lose their faith in adulthood, it is often because they have received poor catechetical instruction. Christian leaders should treat children as fellow seekers who will be no more satisfied with pat answers than adults. Teaching the faith is probably our most difficult task. What children need more than anything else is living faith in Christ. Parents, teachers, and Christian leaders must devote all of their energy and enthusiasm to presenting Christ to their children.[59]

57 Mahlangu, "Theology disrupted," 1–4.

58 Palm, *Scoping*, 61.

59 Bunge, *Child*, 344–6.

Closing Reflections

Reflecting on the popular song, "Jesus Loves me this I know, for the Bible tells me so", this paper set out to explore what the reality of Jesus' love in a fallen and broken world looks like when the child is indeed placed at the centre of how we are church. I reflected on one core reality that children face; violence, asking whether we are affected by such child's presence. I also asked whether the context or position of the child in society and in our churches, move us toward loving such children in how we are church. Through the lens of the discipline of Child Theology, I explored what the Bible does say about the child in our midst and how this influences our theologies of the child. I embraced a liberation theology tool in the CBS methods of biblical interpretation to highlight the impact of centring a child in our reading of the biblical text can make in our understanding of theology but also for the child's faith journey. In what way do we have to change and reformulate our current theological views and faith practices when we revisit them through the eyes and life experiences of children?

Bibliography

Anderson, Cheryl. *Ancient laws and contemporary controversies. The need for inclusive biblical interpretation.* Oxford: Oxford University Press, 2009.

Andrade, Paulo Fernando Carneiro de, Fernando F. Segovia, and Mary Ann Tolbert. "Reading the Bible in the Ecclesial Base Communities of Latin America. The meaning of social context." In *Social location and biblical interpretation in global perspective*, edited by Fernando F. Segovia and Mary Ann Tolbert, vol. 2 of *Reading from this place*. Minneapolis: Fortress Press, 1995, 237–49.

Ansell, Nicola. *Children, youth and development.* London: Routledge, 2016.

Archard, David. *Children: Rights and childhood.* London: Routledge, 2014.

Avest, K. H. ter. "Dutch children and their 'God'. The development of the 'God' concept among indigenous and immigrant children in the Netherlands." *British Journal of Religious Education* 31.3 (2009): 251–62.

Barnett, E. W. "Children and patterns of spiritual growth. A Pauline perspective." United Faculty of Theology, MCDUD, unpublished paper, 2012.

Bunge, Marcia J., ed. *The Child in Christian thought.* Grand Rapids: Eerdmans, 2001.

Caldwell, Elizabeth. "Reading the Bible with Children. Review Essay, Bibles and Bible Story Books." *Religious Education* 110.4 (2015): 452–8.

Collier, John. *Toddling to the Kingdom.* Bangalore: Primalogue Publishing Media, 2008.

Collins, Jennifer. "The contours of 'vulnerability'." In *Vulnerabilities, Care and Family Law*, edited by Julie Wallbank and Jonathan Herrin. London: Routledge, 2013, 22–42.

De Beer, Stephan, and James Genevieve. "Recovering a gospel of love through children. Shattering faith, knowledge and justice." In *Theology, mission and child. Global perspectives*, edited by Bill Prevette, Keith J. White, C. Ewell, and Darren Joseph Konz. Oxford: Regnum, 2014, 78–89.

De Boeck, Filip, and Alcinda Honwana. "Children and youth in Africa. Agency, identity and place: introduction." In *Makers & breakers. Children and youth in postcolonial Africa*. Melton: James Currey, 2005, 1–18.

Dillen, A. "Children between liberation and care. Ethical perspectives on the rights of children and parent-child relationships." *International Journal of Children's Spirituality* 11:2 (2006): 237–50.

Dillen, A. "Religious participation of children as active subjects. Toward a hermeneutical-communicative model of religious education in families with young children." *International Journal of Children's Spirituality* 12:1 (2007): 37–49.

Dillen, A. "The resiliency of children and spirituality. A practical theological reflection." *International Journal of Children's Spirituality* 17:1 (2012): 61–75. DOI: 10.1080/1364436X.2012.67061

Dube, M.W. "Fighting with God. Children and HIV/Aids in Botswana." *Journal of Theology for Southern Africa* 114 (November 2002): 31–42.

Grobbelaar, Jan. *Child theology and the African context*. Child Theology Movement. London: The Child Theology Movement, 2012.

Grobbelaar, Jan, and Chris Jones, eds. *Childhood vulnerabilities in South Africa. Some ethical perspectives*. Melton: African Sun Media, 2021.

Grobbelaar, Jan, and Gert Breed, eds. *Theologies of childhood and the children of Africa*. Cape Town: AOSIS, 2017.

Koopman, Nico. "Public theology and the plight of children in Africa." In *Welcoming Africa's children. Theological and ministry perspectives*, edited by Jan Grobbelaar and Gert Breed. Cape Town: AOSIS, 2016, 193–209.

Mahlangu, Elijah. "Theology disrupted. Doing theology with children in African contexts." *HTS Teologiese Studies/Theological Studies* 72.1 (2016): a3513. http://dx.doi.org/10.4102/hts.v72i1.3513.

Matthaei, Sondra Higgins. "Rethinking faith formation." *Religious Education* 99:1 (2004): 56–70.

Mofokeng, Takatso. "Black Christians, the Bible and liberation." *Journal of black Theology* 2:1 (1988): 34–42.

Mosala, Itumeleng J. and Richard A. Horsley. "A materialist reading of Micah." In *The Bible and Liberation: Political and Social Hermeneutics*, edited by Norman K. Gottwald and Richard A. Horsley. Maryknoll, NY: Orbis Books, 1989, 264–95.

Nessan, Craig L. "Child Liberation Theology." *Currents in Theology and Mission* 45:3 (2018): 6–13.

Oxbrow, Mark. "Christian mission. Contemporary theology and practice with reference to children." In *Theology, mission and child. Global perspectives*, edited by Bill Prevette, Keith J. White, C. Ewell, and Darren Joseph Konz. London: Regnum, 2014, 47–62.

Pais, Janet, *Suffer the children. A theology of liberation by a victim of child abuse.* Mahwah: Paulist Press, 1991.

Pais, M. "Introduction." In *South African child gauge*, edited by Lizette Berry, Linda Biersteker, Andy Dawes, Lori Lake, and Charmaine Smiths. Cape Town: Children's Institute University of Cape Town, 2013.

Palm, Selina. *Scoping study on faith actors' involvement in the prevention, elimination and perpetuation of violence against children.* Expert Consultation Report. JLI EVAC Hub. Accessed 7 October 2023. https://jliflc.com/evac/.

Palm, Selina. "Seen but not heard? Engaging the mechanisms of faith to end violence against children." In *Childhood vulnerabilities in South Africa. Some ethical perspectives*, edited by Jan Grobbelaar and Chris Jones. Stellenbosch: African Sun Media, 2021, 33–64.

Prevette, Bill, Keith J. White, C. Ewell, and Darren Joseph Konz. *Theology, mission and child. Global perspectives.* Oxford: Regnum, 2014.

Punt, Jeremy. "Children's Lives and Agency in the Agonistic First Century and New Testament Studies." *The Thinker* 98:1 (2024): 60–9.

Schneiders, Sandra M. "Feminist ideology criticism and biblical hermeneutics." *Biblical Theology Bulletin* 19:1 (1989): 3–10.

Stoller, R. *Towards a Child liberation theology.* Accessed October 2023. https://rlstollar.com/2015/06/21/towards-a-child-liberation-theology/.

Swart, Ignatius, and Hannelie Yates. "Listening to Africa's children in the process of practical theological interpretation. A South African application." *HTS Teologiese Studies/ Theological Studies* 68:2 (2012): Art. #1310, 12 pages. http://dx.doi.org/10.4102/hts. v68i2.1310.

Trible, Phyllis. "Depatriarchalizing in biblical interpretation." *Journal of the American Academy of Religion* 41:1 (1973), 30–48.

United Nations International Children's Emergency Fund (UNICEF). *The state of the world's children 2006.* https://www.unicef.org/media/84806/file/SOWC-2006.pdf.

Weber, Shantelle, and Stephan De Beer. "Doing theology with children in a South African context. Children as collaborators in intergenerational ministry." *HTS Teologiese Studies/ Theological Studies* 72:1 (2016): a3572. http://dx.doi. org/10.4102/hts.v72i1.3572.

West, Gerald O. "And the Dumb Do Speak. Articulating Incipient Readings of the Bible in Marginalized Communities." In *The Bible in Ethics*, edited by J.W.

Rogerson, M. Davies, and R. Carroll. Sheffield: Sheffield Academic Press, 1995, 174–92.

West, Gerald O. "Locating 'Contextual Bible Study' within biblical liberation hermeneutics and intercultural biblical hermeneutics." *HTS Teologiese Studies/ Theological Studies* 70:1 (2014): Art. #2641, 10 pages. http://dx.doi.org/10.4102/hts.v70i1.2641.

Wit, Hans de, L. Jonker, M. Kool, and D. Schipani. *Through the eyes of another. Intercultural reading of the Bible.* Amsterdam: Institute of Mennonite Studies, 2004.

Amsterdam University Press

YEARBOOK OF CONTEXTUAL BIBLICAL INTERPRETATION 1 (2024) 27-45
HTTPS://DOI.ORG/10.5117/YCBI2024.003.NAGE

Seeing and Experiencing Things Differently. How the Theologizing of Children Can Contribute to Theology

C.H. (Corina) Nagel-Herweijer, freelance trainer, consultant, writer and developer in the field of Youth Ministry and Religious Education, PhD candidate at the Protestant Theological University in the Netherlands. cnagelherweijer@student.pthu.nl

P.M. (Ronelle) Sonnenberg, associate professor Practical Theology at the Protestant Theological University in the Netherlands and research associate Practical Theology and Missiology at the Theological Faculty of Stellenbosch University. pmsonnenberg@pthu.nl

Abstract
In this article, we provide a conceptual clarification of the terms "child theology" and "children's theology" on the basis of a literature review. This allows us to position our question "how children's theology can contribute to theology" well within the academic debate on the subject. We take up the social constructivism that is the underlying paradigm of children's theology, and we do so in a way that explicitly includes God as an actor. It is our argument that, due to their developmental stage, they are capable of offering perspectives that are complementary to those of expert theologians. The perspectives they offer depend on the context in which they grow up. Two examples of a practice illustrate the argument as to how children can contribute to theology.

Keywords: Child theology, children's theology, God-Talk, social constructivism, developmental stage

Introduction

> *Last Sunday, the children returned from Sunday school to the church with their drawings. Among them I saw some drawings of God with a beard on a cloud. Terrible! I always doubted the level of Sunday school, but now I know for sure that there is no quality at all.*
> Pastor of a local perish

> *Of course, we cannot just let children read the Bible book of Jonah. It is one of the most complex books of the Old Testament. It requires a lot of background knowledge to understand this book properly.*
> Assistant Professor in theology

These two examples from 2023 suggest a pattern of faith formation in which faith appears to be transmitted from adults to children, with the latter often perceived as passive recipients. Other examples could be added to further support this potential paradigm. This paradigm posits that the theology of children is less mature and of a lower order than that of adults, including parents, teachers, and academic theologians. This perspective has been dominant for a considerable period of time.[1] In the present era, a novel paradigm is gaining prominence. Within the domain of youth ministry, this paradigm currently represents the dominant framework through which the process of faith formation is conceptualized.[2] It posits that children are not mere passive recipients of faith; rather, they are encouraged to engage with it actively, exploring their own interpretations of events and religious texts. Within this paradigm, children are supported in developing their own understanding of faith and are encouraged to discover new answers to age-old questions. It challenges the traditional image of educators as omniscient figures, instead portraying them as learners alongside the children.[3] This paradigm aligns with social constructivism,[4] which is a significant learning theory in youth ministry and in education.[5]

1 Bucher, "Kindertheologie," 9; Miedema, "Overdracht of toe-eigening," 75–9; Roebben, *Godsdienstpedagogiek*, 28–30.

2 De Kock and Norheim, *The Five Questions*, 236.

3 Alii, *Godsdienstpedagogiek*, 110–13; Ipgrave, "My God"; Miedema, "Overdracht of toe-eigening," 79–83.

4 Brieden, "Konstruktivistische Religionsdidaktik"; Roose and Büttner, "Epistemological Framework".

5 Bickhard, "Constructivisms and Relativisms"; Woolfolk, Hughes, and Walkup, *Psychology*, 396–435.

This new paradigm is one that we support. In the context of children's faith formation, it is of the utmost importance to provide them with the opportunity to engage in theological reflection. Firstly, this approach respects the unique spiritual nature of each child. Secondly, it enables them to examine their own presuppositions, which in turn fosters a deeper understanding of complex concepts such as morality, justice, and spirituality. Such exploration also nurtures a sense of autonomy and agency in their religious and ethical development.[6]

It is undeniable that theologizing plays an essential role in children's growth and maturity. However, it raises the question: does the theologizing of children also hold significance for the field of theology itself? This article delves into this issue, addressing the question of how children's theologizing contributes to theology, understood as "theo-logy" or "God-talk".[7]

Child Theology and Children's Theology

In order to respond to the central question, we will focus our attention on a particular movement within constructivist religious pedagogy, the paradigm we described above. It is somewhat confusing that two concepts are used within this approach, which are also occasionally used interchangeably. The following paragraphs will explain these different concepts and show where they correspond and differ. Both concepts are useful for the question of how children can contribute to theology. The first concept is "child theology". The second is "children's theology", also called "theologizing with children".

Child Theology

The presentation by Weber on November 1, 2023, focused on "child theology", which is represented by the Child Theology Movement and has its roots in the Anglo-Saxon world.[8] It seeks to consider central themes of theology (whether historical, biblical, or systematic) in the light of the child standing beside Jesus amid the disciples (Matt. 18:1–5). This child functions as a lens

6 Bucher, "Kindertheologie"; Schweitzer, "Kindertheologie."

7 This article is based on our reactions (both academic and professional) to the presentation of Shantelle Weber at the conference on November 1, 2023. It contains a conceptual exploration and illustrates, with the aid of two examples drawn from one of the author's own experience, what children's theology is about.

8 Cf. White and Willmer, *Introduction*; Mountain, "Four Links".

through which certain aspects of God and his revelation can be observed with greater clarity. Child theology serves to rectify the marginalization or invisibility of children in mainstream theological discourse, advocating for the inclusion of children in theological reflection and practice.[9] The movement identifies four qualities of children's spirituality that can facilitate adults' access to "life in all its fullness" or the "Kingdom of God": living based in relationship, living in vulnerability, living in creativity and play, and living in openness and hope.[10]

As colleague Weber correctly asserts (see the preceding chapter in this volume), an emphasis on the agency of children represents a perspective within the broader discourse of liberation theology. The question of agency or "agentive participation", pertains to the ways in which children navigate social norms, practices, and content, as well as the extent to which they adopt and adapt these elements. What responsibilities are assigned to them? What is their contribution to the culture with which they are associated?[11]

Children's Theology

The concept "theologizing with children" or "children's theology" is closely related to "child theology". It has its origins in Germany. Similarly, it regards children as active agents and spiritual subjects. However, "child theology" is concerned with how adults perceive and interpret children's perceptions, experiences, and actions. Consequently, adults are the primary actors. In contrast to "child theology", "children's theology" places a stronger emphasis on the process of meaning-making by children, on children creating theology. In this context, children are the primary actors.[12] "Child theology" is primarily a perspective through which children are observed and appreciated. In contrast, children's theology is a methodology that shapes learning processes with children. Both approaches originate from a similar premise, namely that children should be regarded as partners in a dialogue.

As outlined by Roebben,[13] "children's theology" is founded upon three fundamental principles. Primarily, it espouses the recognition of the fundamental dignity of every child. The tenets of children's theology include

9 White and Willmer, *Introduction*.

10 Mountain, "Four Links," 265–68.

11 Van Leersum-Bekebrede, *Worship*, 63, 75.

12 Sagberg, "Children," 113; Sommer, Pramling Samuelsson, and Hundeide, *Child Perspectives*, vi.

13 Roebben, "Children's Theology," 14–16.

the conviction that every child possesses an intrinsic dignity as a peculiar and irreplaceable human being. All humans possess an inalienable right to be small, vulnerable, and in a state of development. Conversely, each child has its own voice through which theology is expressed. Secondly, children's theology can be viewed as a postmodern way approach to theology, according to which faith is only considered valid when it is personally embraced. Thirdly, the debates between content and competence, handing over and discovering, and content-centered and child-centered approaches are resolved dialectically.

The triad is a distinctive feature of children's theology. It encompasses theologizing of, with and for children, as initially conceptualized by Schweitzer.[14] Currently, the triad is employed extensively in both descriptive and prescriptive learning contexts.[15] This brief exposition elucidates the triad.

> *Theologizing of children*: the cognitive processes through which children engage with religious thoughts, ideas, presumptions, etc. Adults are attentive to the religious expressions of children.
>
> *Theologizing with children*: children explore answers to theological questions in collaborations with adults, who serve as their equal partners in the process, but with different input.
>
> *Theologizing for children*: The nurturer or educator facilitates children's development by imparting theological knowledge and personal beliefs that enable them to progress towards the zone of proximal development.[16]

From our perspective, the aimed synthesis or complementarity of the triad is the beauty of children's theology. The three elements are given their full weight. Each component of the triad is constrained by its own limitations;[17] however, collectively they foster communication and understanding between

14 Schweitzer, "Was ist und wozu Kindertheologie?"

15 Büttner, Schreiner, Freudenberger-Lötz, Kalloch, *Theologisieren*; Freudenberger-Lötz, *Theologische Gespräche*; Hutter and Kuindersma, *Nooit meer een kleurplaat*; Zimmermann, "What Is Children's Theology?".

16 The Zone of Proximal Development (ZPD) represents a fundamental tenet within Lev Vygotsky's theoretical framework concerning learning and developmental processes. The ZPD is defined as the area between the capabilities a learner can achieve independently and the capabilities they can achieve with the support of an adult or in collaboration with more proficient peers. Vygotsky, *Mind*, 86.

17 Zimmermann, "What Is Children's Theology?," 3.

generations. The theologizing of children affords them a full voice in intergenerational dialogue, and their theologizing is as valuable as that of adults. Theologizing is not limited to adults or even more specifically professionals but given to children too. At the same time, their development is not possible without the guidance of others. They need "experts" who can introduce and initiate them to theological themes and language. Finally, they require encounters, dialogues, confrontations, enrichment, and mutual wonders from adults who facilitate their journey of theological meaning-making. This triad balances intergenerational youth ministry.

Theologizing of Children

While the triad of theologizing of, with, and for children is a hallmark of children's theology, and we have previously underscored its merits, the remainder of this article will concentrate on the theologizing of children and its value for theology.

Providing children with the space to theologize not only fosters their personal religious growth but also creates an opportunity for them to contribute to the development of theological discourse. Their uninhibited and open way of life helps adults embrace transcendence and the Mystery of life in a new way. They can facilitate a reconnection with spirituality in adults who may have lost some of their connection to it.[18]

Moreover, children can also uncover meanings that adults may not be aware of. This is effectively demonstrated in a small-scale action research study conducted by Roose and Butt.[19] A series of three lessons based on the parable of the unforgiving servant from Matt. 18:21–35 was developed for pupils aged nine and ten. This biblical passage recounts the story of a servant who owes a significant debt to a king, and the king subsequently cancels the debt. Upon leaving, the servant encounters another servant who owes him a much smaller debt and is unable to pay it. The first servant then imprisons the second servant. When the king hears of this, he becomes enraged and punishes the first servant severely.

The parable presents a challenge for exegetes, particularly in regard to the discrepancy between the king's actions in the first and third scenes. One particularly challenging aspect for exegetes is the harshness of the king's actions in the third scene. In contrast, the children in the study

18 Roebben, "Children's Theology," 15.

19 Roose and Butt, "God Cannot Always Forgive."

considered the king's actions towards the first servant in the third scene to be justified. They believe that God is a loving deity who only judges when necessary to prevent evil.

Roose and Butt[20] posit that children, through their interpretation of this parable, bring attention to the interpretive framework of adults when reading the Bible. Specifically, the adult's identification with the first servant, their need for unending forgiveness, and their fear of an unforgiving God may be more reflective of Lutheran theology than of biblical theology itself. This illustrates how children can challenge adults' assumptions and contribute to theological discourse.

In order to do justice to theologizing of children and to utilize their voices to enrich theology, it is essential to consider two key aspects, which will be elaborated upon in the following two paragraphs. Firstly, we reflect on the phase of childhood in relation to the meaning-making of children. Secondly, context and personal particularity matter. We refer to the study of David Csinos,[21] who draws attention to the universalist, cultural, and individual dimension of theological meaning-making of children.

Phase of Childhood in Relation to Theological Meaning-aking

Children experience, think, and witness the world in different ways than adults do, as is explained by several developmental models (Piaget, Kohlberg, Erickson, Fowler).[22] It is not a concern for preschoolers with their magical perspective that Jonah was in the fish for several days, while the same Bible passage prompts significant reflection for teenagers. Children between the ages of 10 and 12, often referred to as the "betweeners", are capable of logical thought and therefore have a tendency to dwell on questions of origin. Teenagers' cognitive development progresses from concrete to abstract, and then to personalistic. During this period, questioning the truth is a crucial aspect of their learning process. As adolescents look at reality from a multidimensional perspective, these questions are less important for them.[23]

The developmental psychology of children and adolescents is evident in their perception of God. It is common for young children to conceptualize God in a highly anthropomorphic manner, viewing him as a bearded

20 Roose and Butt, "God Cannot Always Forgive," 49.

21 Csinos, *Little Theologians*.

22 Cf. Alii, *Godsdienstpedagogiek*; Paloutzian, *Invitation*.

23 Cf. Nagel-Herweijer, Sonnenberg, and Groen, *Dat je groeien mag*, 37–8, 80–2.

man seated on a cloud. As children mature, they begin to conceptualize God in a more abstract way, for instance depicting him as having multiple arms or eyes or portraying a female figure as God. When questioned about their conception of God, teenagers primarily respond through symbolic representations.[24]

Children's theology fully honors children with their childlike worldview. Anthropomorphic images of God are not an expression of deficiency but are just as valuable as abstract and multifaceted images of God. Children have the right to read and interpret Bible stories in a magical way.[25] Bucher calls this the first naivety.[26] According to him, this does not mean ignorance, but above all an openness and an immediate oneness with realities that for most adults have been emptied into fictions, such as magical figures like guardian angels or Santa Claus. The value of first naivety does not mean that we should fixate on it or infantilize children, nor that adults should imitate it. But the metaphysical truth that children can experience contributes to theology. They have a right to educators who will listen to them and try to understand them, and from there give them appropriate guidance. It can be argued that developmental psychological differences lead to a complementary perspective between children and professional theologians.[27]

Three Spheres of Human Life

Csinos studied the theological meaning making of children.[28] In his ethnographic study, these children belong to churches, but the same method can be used with other groups. He wanted to know *if and how the participation of children in a particular congregation influences the process of theological meaning-making.* He therefore interviewed nineteen children from four different United Church of Canada congregations. In the interviews, which took place in 2013 and 2014, he began by inviting the children to draw a picture of God. This method of drawing is often used in studies of children and has been shown to be valuable. Drawing provides non-verbal access to children's inner lives.[29] He interviewed children between the ages of 5

24 Maull, *Gottesbilder*; Schlange, *Die Entwicklung*; Schweitzer, *Kindertheologie*, 134–48.

25 Bucher, "Kindertheologie," 20.

26 Bucher, "Kindertheologie," 11.

27 Bucher, "Kindertheologie," 11; Roose and Butt, "God Cannot Always Forgive," 41.

28 Csinos, *Little Theologians*.

29 E.g., Cox, "Intention and Meaning"; Schweitzer, *Kindertheologie*, 134–48.

and 13 years old and he interviewed a group of adults (including leaders, parents, and volunteers) in each congregation. He created a portrait of four congregations: a culturally diverse congregation, an ethnic minority congregation, an ethnic majority congregation and an Aboriginal congregation. He included in his sample a variety of contextual factors, like urban and rural, size, and beliefs. Consequently, the concept of culture in this study is not limited to language and ethnicity but encompasses a multitude of factors. In the individual or small group (two or three) interviews with the children, the process of drafting as well as the drafts themselves, became the starting point for the further conversation with the children about God, church, heaven, and whatever theological topics the children brought up.

Csinos[30] used the trinitarian theory of the intercultural theologian Lartey[31] on the distinction of a universalist, cultural, and individual sphere of human life. Csinos constructed a clear and convincing narrative of all three in relation to the theological meaning making of the children. The first sphere, universalist, covers the overall aspect. For example, all children could describe something about God. Which means there was some literacy. And in all the congregations the theological meaning making of children is influenced by participating in the congregation. The sources are implicit or explicit theological convictions, like place for uncertainty in faith (a), or experiences like communal events as retreats and meals (b), or relationships in the congregation that incarnate a theology of love (c). While all children utilize these sources, they do so to varying degrees. The second sphere, that of culture, encompasses notions that are shared with others within a particular congregation. They are characteristic of a particular congregation and do not relate to the others as the universalist meaning does. Here, the cultural influence comes forward. For example, the influence of a particular camp experience is characteristic in the theological meaning making of a particular group. The final sphere, individual, pertains to the specific experiences and perceptions of an individual, such as a distinctive experience like a certain dream. It should be noted that these factors can also be related to cultural influences. However, in the interviews, the meaning was related to the particularity of the individual. Theological meaning-making, in the sense of "theo-logos", is, as Csinos' study demonstrates, a capacity that can be exhibited by any child within the church. However, in engaging in this process, every child is shaped by the congregation they belong to in

30 Csinos, *Little Theologians*.

31 Lartey, *In Living Color*.

their construction of theological meaning. In addition to personal factors, cultural influences play a role in theological meaning-making.

From a theological perspective we add one extra layer, namely that God must come in action to constitute knowledge of God.[32] As we understand theology and theologizing, not only humans are actors, but God could also be, in a mediated way.

> Revelation as a free divine activity is an objective category, but it is also a very subjective category of the recognition of revelation in human experience that decides whether the free offer of divine grace will be accepted.[33]

Children's Wisdom: Two Examples of the Theologizing of Children

To answer the question of how children can contribute to theology, in addition to the literature review, we introduce two examples in which children theologize. We will explain how their theologizing contributes to theological understanding. The first case study involved an initial learning process that was carefully designed. The second case study emerged spontaneously. Both cases were observed in our own teaching and parenting practices, and they have provided us with valuable insights into the process of theological reflection with children.

Spiritual Growth at School

The first case was at a public primary school where I [CN] was a religious teacher. One of the groups I taught was a group with all gifted pupils. On occasion, I utilized the Godly Play method in this class. This method is aligned with the "children's theology" school of thought. It is worth noting that this method incorporates so-called wondering questions, which are posed to the children after a bible story has been narrated. These wondering questions serve to create a space for creative engagement with the biblical narrative presented.[34]

32 Van den Brink and Van der Kooi, *Christelijke dogmatiek*, 50.
33 Štěch, "Fundamental Theology," 86.
34 Berryman, "Theologizing with Children."

During the lesson, I sat with my pupils in a circle on the ground and told the story of *The faces of Easter*.[35] The story is structured around eight pivotal moments in Jesus' life, commencing with his birth and concluding with his resurrection. I inquired as to which part of the narrative they found most appealing. One of them reacted: "I like the part of Jesus birth best. Because without his birth, all the other things wouldn't have happened either." Another boy replied, "I like the part of the resurrection best." He then literally repeated a phrase I used during the storytelling, "The end is a beginning too," and leaned back to think about it. I looked around the circle to see if any other child wanted to respond. One of the pupils bent forward to touch the picture that accompanied the part of the story he liked best.

> I like the part in which Jesus was as a twelve-year-old boy in the temple best. I also know a lot, often much more than other children, and I enjoy talking to adults. But just like Jesus, I notice that people often do not understand me. I really find that difficult sometimes.

Others responded with recognition. "Yes, I find that difficult too. Then kids laugh at me, or adults tell me not to interfere." The pupil who first spoke about Jesus in the temple took the floor again: "Jesus did not let it upset him. He continued to do what he believed he should do. I want that too." Most of the other children nodded in agreement.

Children are often vulnerable. When you are different from others, in this case, because of giftedness, you are even more vulnerable. Theologizing about this story had a positive effect on the pupils' spirituality, particularly the twelve years old Jesus, who inspired them. Furthermore, the pupils' unique perspective and background as gifted students prompted me to view this familiar Bible passage in a new light. This also contributed to my own spiritual growth. This is precisely the outcome that Godly Play aims to achieve.[36]

The cognitive development theories (Piaget and others) and faith development theories (Fowler) do not focus on special gifted people. To take these people seriously one should not only look at their age and whether they are in the phase of mythic-literal or synthetic-conventional,[37] but also at their social-emotional development, as is argued by many others.[38] The

35 Berryman, *Complete Guide*, Lesson 2–8.

36 Berryman, *Teaching*.

37 Alii, *Godsdienstpedagogiek*, 143; Paloutzian, *Invitation*, 179.

38 E.g., Alii, *Godsdienstpedagogiek*, 148 ff.

perspective of role-taking includes social-emotional development, as the aforementioned vignette illustrates. In addition to serving as an educator for the rabbis, Jesus also serves as a role model (which a teacher might be) for these gifted children. By listening to the theological meaning-making of these children, we noticed how in interpreting this story, vulnerability and strength, spiritually interact. Furthermore, adults are able to gain renewed access to this story through the theological interpretation provided by children. It should be noted that this vignette is not based on a comprehensive contextual investigation, as in Csinos'[39] study, so we cannot make contextual claims here, but it also shows us that children in a public-school setting are able to theologize and that individual characteristics influence this theologizing. Furthermore, it becomes clear that these young children can position themselves towards their context in their own way.

Blessed at Home

As a mother, I [CN] regularly read from the Bible with my toddlers, aged 1 and 3. The children like the "Baby Bible"[40] best. This bible was also inspired by children's theology. It fits well with the development of babies and toddlers: their sensory need, need for safety, and curiosity, constantly imitating the others around them.[41] Each bible story in this Bible concludes with a song.

We read the story of Jesus, who blessed the children. It is one of the children's favorites. When I demonstrated that Jesus was saying that people may come to him, the children enthusiastically joined me. When we read that a man said that the children were not allowed to come to Jesus, we all looked angry and signed to stop. After we read the story, we sang the song, and we performed it with gestures. In the second verse we sang:

Come along, He gives you His blessing
Come along, His hand on your head.
He is with you, in sun and rain
He does what He has promised you
Come along, He'll give you His blessing
Come along, His hand on your head.

39 Csinos, *Little Theologians.*

40 Oranje and Ten Berge, *Baby.*

41 Hutter and Kuindersma, *Nooit meer een kleurplaat*, 113–18.

Every time we sang that Jesus blesses them or lays his hand on their head, I put my hand on the heads of my children. They liked it and laughed together. The last time, my three-year-old son imitated me. He put his hand on my head.

I go to church every Sunday. At the end of the service, I receive God's blessing. I have become used to it, so it doesn't always affect me. However, that morning, Jesus blessed me through my son's hands at the messy kitchen table. It had been a long time since I had felt it so strongly. We switched roles. My son brought Jesus to me after I brought my children to Jesus.

This case study demonstrates how the act of imitating, which encompasses both theologizing for and of children, can lead to a reversal of roles and theologizing with children. This dynamic interplay between roles creates an opportunity for God to speak in an unexpected way, also to adults. In children's theology, the focus is not only on the actors and theologians, but also on how God acts and reveals himself through our God-talk and how through God-talk of children, adults can get inspired. God is mediated in embodied and discursive practices. In line with Firet, the emphasis might be placed on the coming of God. The Word is not just a word: coming occurs.[42] Words, acts, and substances are embedded in a concrete and contextual setting and "as such they are empirical phenomena but also open to a metaphysical or a theological *more* because they engage participants and because of engagement of participants."[43]

Conclusion and Discussion

The central question in this article is: how does children's theologizing contribute to theology, in the sense of "theo-logy" or "God-talk"? The theoretical exploration of the concepts "child theology" and "children's theology" demonstrates that the use of these concepts is contingent upon the context where it is used. In the Netherlands, our primary reference point is the German context. In Germany, the prevailing concepts differ from those observed in other countries, such as the USA or Norway. Moreover, the concepts are frequently employed in a combined manner in literature, without sufficient clarification. The conceptual exploration demonstrates that the term "children's theology" encompasses the broader conceptual field of "child theology", while focusing on the perspective and learning of children.

42 Firet, *Dynamics*, 39–40.

43 Sonnenberg, *Youth Worship*, 176.

This article sets out two keyways in which children contribute to theology, drawing on both academic literature and practitioner experience. Firstly, children's spirituality, which is characterized by openness, receptivity and playfulness, contributes to the spirituality of adults. They assist adults in showing other perspectives of spirituality that adults might have lost touch with. This can be done with both "ordinary" believers and theologians. Secondly, children's unique childish approach can highlight areas of weakness in theology, or alternatively, provide new insights through their original perspectives.

The assumption that children can contribute to theology implies that they have a voice, as evidenced by the prominence of child theology and children's theology. This voice is understood both literally and figuratively. Children literally express themselves through the use of a specific theological language. Additionally, they have a distinct "voice" in how they engage with and adopt various aspects of faith, including practices and beliefs. Consequently, children's theologizing plays a pivotal role in the evolution of theology. The notion of God-Talk is not exclusive to adults. In alignment with the tenets of liberation theology, Children's theologizing democratizes (the concept of) theology.

How the children's voice sounds or what it says is influenced by the (faith) community to which the child belongs as well as by individual characteristics, such as their developmental stage. Here is where intercultural theology (cf. Larteys[44]), developmental psychology (cf. Bucher[45]), and youth ministry (cf. Csinos[46]) intersect.

Narratives, practices, and experience are at the heart of this theologizing with children. Professionals and part of the adults have access to theological higher order concepts of a particular tradition, but everyone has access to imagination, existential experiences and questions, as well as stories. That is where generations encounter each other in children's theology. This also implies that children's theologizing adds an intergenerational dimension to theology.

While it is true that children can contribute to the development of theology through theologizing, this does not automatically lead to the growth and advancement of the children themselves. This article focuses on the topic of children theologizing. However, it is insufficient for the development of children's faith to solely listen to their own voice. It is vital that they have

44 Lartey, *In Living Color.*

45 Bucher, "Kindertheologie."

46 Csinos, *Little Theologians.*

the opportunity to expand and challenge their perspectives by engaging with a diverse range of voices, both contemporary and historical, in both oral and written forms. It is essential that educators are able to engage with children in a theological discourse. This allows children to gain a deeper understanding of their educators' knowledge and explore their own perspectives and those of others, thus fostering their own meaning-making process.[47] By engaging the full triad of children's theology within learning processes, we can value the human references to God of children and their educators while also critically encountering human interpretations. Both the testimony and interpretations of the children and their educators must be thoroughly examined[48] to understand Gods voice in our God-Talk. From an epistemological perspective, interpretations in human communication also by children, and its references to God must be taken seriously, however, not as a direct uncritical link to the metaphysics but in a critical way.[49] This means the voices, or more theologically said, the witnesses of children and adults must be tested as well. Integrity is important here: does someone really mean what he or she says and is there integrity in someone's attitude to others? Does acting resonate with the witness? Furthermore, testimonies should be compared to the testimony of what has been accepted as word of God by previous generations.[50] So, God-Talk also in Children's theology is not 1:1 the same as God's talk to us, but it might reveal God's talk. However, to discern this, critical examination is needed as well. And it is this cohesion of voices in Children's theology, that includes a critical examination by comparing voices of children and adults.

We commenced this article with two concise examples that occurred within the past year. Consider the scenario in which the pastor engages in conversation with the child whom God has depicted as a man on a cloud. As an alternative scenario, consider the case of the assistant professor leading a discussion on the book of Jonah with a group of children without providing them with extensive prior information. What would have been the outcome? Such an encounter might have led to a deeper understanding of God on the part of the preacher, or it might have revealed a previously unnoticed aspect of the Jonah story to the assistant professor. Was that the end of the conversation? From our perspective, this was not the case. By asking questions and providing context, the children could have tested and broadened their own

47 Roose and Butt, "God Cannot Always Forgive."
48 Sonnenberg, *Youth Worship*, 163.
49 Sonnenberg, *Youth Worship*, 163.
50 Korpel and De Moor, *Silent*, 298.

perspectives. Unfortunately, this dialogue never materialized because the importance of the children's voices was not recognized by the theologians. Consequently, we are unable to determine how much knowledge both the children and the theologians would have gained from this encounter. This is not only a missed opportunity for the development of children, but also for the development of theology.

Bibliography

Alii, E. T. *Godsdienstpedagogiek. Dimensies en spanningsvelden.* Zoetermeer: Uitgeverij Meinema, 2009.

Berryman, Jerome W. *Teaching Godly Play. How to Mentor the Spiritual Development of Children.* New York: Morehouse Education Resources, 2009.

Berryman, Jerome W. *The Complete Guide to Godly Play.* Volume 4, revised and expanded. New York: Church Publishing, 2018.

Berryman, Jerome W. "Theologizing with Children: A Parable Approach." In *Hovering over the Face of the Deep. Philosophy, Theology and Children*, edited by Gertrud Yde Iversen, Gordon Mitchell, and Gaynor Pollard. Münster, New York, München, Berlin: Waxmann Verlag, 2009, 197–214.

Bickhard, Mark H. "Constructivisms and Relativisms: A Shopper's Guide." *Science & Education* 6:1 (1997): 29–42. https://doi.org/10.1023/A:1008636107835.

Brieden, Norbert. "Konstruktivistische Religionsdidaktik 2.0." In *Religionsunterricht weiterdenken. Innovative Ansätze für eine zukunftsfähige Religionsdidakti*, edited by Bernard Grümme and Manfred L. Pirner. Stuttgart: Kohlhammer, 2023, 29–44.

Brink, G. van den, and C. van der Kooi. *Christelijke dogmatiek.* Zoetermeer: Boekencentrum, 2011.

Bucher, Anton. "Kindertheologie: Provokation? Romantizismus? Neues Paradigma." In *"Mittendrin ist Gott". Kinder denken nach über Gott, Leben und Tod*, edited by Anton Bucher, Gerhard Büttner, Petra Freudenberger-Lötz, and Martin Schreiner. Jahrbuch für Kindertheologie. Vol. 1. Stuttgart: Calwer, 2008, 9–27.

Büttner, Gerhard, Martin Schreiner, Petra Freudenberger-Lötz, and Christina Kalloch, eds. *Handbuch Theologisieren mit Kindern: Einführung – Schlüsselthemen – Methoden.* Stuttgart: Calwer Verlag / Kösel Verlag, 2014.

Cox, Sue. "Intention and Meaning in Young Children's Drawing." *International Journal of Art & Design Education* 24:2 (2005): 115–25. https://doi.org/10.1111/j.1476-8070.2005.00432.x.

Csinos, David M. *Little Theologians. Children, Culture, and the Making of Theological Meaning.* Montreal: McGill-Queen's University Press, 2020.

Firet, Jacob J. *Dynamics in Pastoring.* Grand Rapids: Eerdmans, 1986.

Freudenberger-Lötz, Petra. *Theologische Gespräche mit Kindern. Untersuchungen zur Professionalisierung Studierender und Anstöße zu forschendem Lernen im Religionsunterricht.* Stuttgart: Calwer Verlag, 2007.

Hutter, Maartien, and Henk Kuindersma. *Nooit meer een kleurplaat. Raak geïnspireerd door kindertheologie.* Haarlem: Nederlands-Vlaams Bijbelgenootschap, 2021.

Ipgrave, Julia. "'My God and Other People's Gods'. Children's Theology in a Context of Plurality," In *Hovering over the Face of the Deep. Philosophy, Theology and Children*, edited by Gertrud Yde Iversen, Gordon Mitchell, and Gaynor Pollard. Münster, New York, München, Berlin: Waxmann Verlag, 2009, 53–69.

Kock, Jos de, and Bård Norheim. *The Five Questions. An Academic Handbook in Youth Ministry Research*/ Eugene, OR: Pickwick Publications, 2022.

Korpel, Marjo C. A., and Johannes C. De Moor. *The Silent God.* Leiden: Brill, 2011.

Lartey, Emmanuel Yartekwei. *In Living Color. An Intercultural Approach to Pastoral Care and Counseling.* London, New York: Jessica Kingsley Publishers, 2003.

Leersum-Bekebrede, Lydia van. *Worship with Children. Agentive Participation in Dutch Protestant Contexts.* Amsterdam Protestant Theological University, 2021. https://doi.org/10.21827/61a0b3d27e7af.

Maull, Ibtissame Yasmine. *Gottesbilder und Gottesvorstellungen vom Kindes- zum Jugendalter. Eine qualitativ-empirische Längsschnittuntersuchung.* Göttingen: Vandenhoeck & Ruprecht, 2017.

Miedema, Siebren. "Overdracht of toe-eigening? Over wat je je kinderen wilt meegeven." In *Alle onderwijs bijzonder. Levensbeschouwelijke waarden in het onderwijs*, edited by Siebren Miedema and Henk Vroom. Zoetermeer: Meinema, 2002, 73–96.

Mountain, Vivienne. "Four Links between Child Theology and Children's Spirituality." *International Journal of Children's Spirituality*, 16:3 (2011): 261–69. https://doi.org/10.1080/1364436X.2011.617729.

Nagel-Herweijer, Corina, Ronelle Sonnenberg, and Eduard Groen. *Dat je groeien mag! Een casestudy naar de wijze waarop jongeren binnen de Protestantse Kerk in Nederland leren geloven.* Utrecht: Protestantse Kerk in Nederland, 2023. Accessed March 12, 2024. https://protestantsekerk.nl/nieuws/nieuw-onderzoek-geeft-antwoord-op-de-vraag-hoe-jongeren-leren-geloven/.

Oranje, Corien, and Marieke Ten Berge. *Baby Bijbel.* Haarlem: Nederlands Bijbelgenootschap, 2019.

Paloutzian, Raymond F. *Invitation to the Psychology of Religion.* 3rd edition. New York: Guilford Press, 2016.

Roebben, Bert. *Godsdienstpedagogiek van de hoop. Grondlijnen voor religieuze vorming.* Leuven: Acco, 2007.

Roebben, Bert. "Children's Theology. Concepts and Contexts, Problems and Horizons." In *Symmetrical Communication? Philosophy and Theology in Classrooms across Europe*, edited by Friedhelm Kraft, Hanna Roose, and Gerhard Büttner. Rehburg-Loccum: RPI Loccum, 2011, 11–24.

Roose, Hanna, and Christian Butt. "'God Cannot Always Forgive'. Reading Mt 18:21-35 with Children." In *Hovering over the Face of the Deep. Philosophy, Theology and Children*, edited by Gertrud Yde Iversen, Gordon Mitchell, and Gaynor Pollard. Münster, New York, München, Berlin: Waxmann Verlag, 2009, 37–53.

Roose, Hanna, and Gerhard Büttner. "The Epistemological Framework for Theologizing with Children. Critical Realism or Social Constructivism? A Response to Andrew Wright." In *Hovering over the Face of the Deep. Philosophy, Theology and Children*, edited by Gertrud Yde Iversen, Gordon Mitchell, and Gaynor Pollard. Münster, New York, München, Berlin: Waxmann Verlag, 2009, 177–84.

Sagberg, Sturla. "Children as Spiritual Subjects and the Significance of Educational Environments." In *Symmetrical Communication? Philosophy and Theology in Classrooms across Europe*, edited by Friedhelm Kraft, Hanna Roose, and Gerhard Büttner. Loccum: Religionspädagogisches Institut Loccum, 2011, 113–32.

Schlange, Christina. *Die Entwicklung von Gottesbildern bei Kindern unter Berücksichtigung ihrer religiösen Sozialisation. Eine Untersuchung im Blick auf Schülerinnen und Schüler der dritten und vierten Jahrgangsstufe*. Münster: Westfälische Wilhems-Universität Münster, 2011.

Schweitzer, Friedrich. *Kindertheologie und Elementarisierung. Wie religiöses Lernen mit Kindern gelingen kann*. Gütersloh: Gütersloher Verlagshaus, 2011.

Schweitzer, Friedrich. "Was ist und wozu Kindertheologie?" In *"Im Himmelreich ist keiner sauer": Kinder als Exegeten*, edited by Anton Bucher, Gerhard Büttner, Petra Freudenberger-Lötz, and Martin Schreiner. Jahrbuch für Kindertheologie 2. Stuttgart: Calwer Verlag, 2003), 9–18.

Sommer, Dion, Ingrid Pramling Samuelsson, and Karsten Hundeide. *Child Perspectives and Children's Perspectives in Theory and Practice*. Dordrecht: Springer Netherlands, 2010.

Sonnenberg, Ronelle. *Youth Worship in Protestant Contexts. A Practical Theological Theory of Participation of Adolescents*. Amsterdam: Protestant Theological University, 2015.

Štěch, František. "Fundamental Theology, Dynamics of Christian Life and Identity." *ET-Studies* 5:1 (2014): 77–95.

Vygotsky, L. S. *Mind in Society. The Development of Higher Psychological Processes*. Edited by Michael Cole, Vera John-Steiner, Sylvia Scribner, and Ellen Souberman. Revised edition. Cambridge, MA: Harvard University Press, 1978.

White, Keith J., and Haddon Willmer. *An Introduction to Child Theology*. Key Topics in Child Theology, Series 1. Valparaiso: The Child Theology Movement, 2006.

Woolfolk, Anita, Malcolm Hughes, and Vivienne Walkup. *Psychology in Education*. Harlow: Pearson Longman, 2008.

Zimmermann, Mirjam. "What Is Children's Theology? Children's Theology as Theological Competence. Development, Differentiation, Methods." *HTS Teologiese Studies/Theological Studies* 71:3 (2015): 1–6. https://doi.org/10.4102/hts.v71i3.2848.

Amsterdam University Press

YEARBOOK OF CONTEXTUAL BIBLICAL INTERPRETATION 1 (2024) 46-56
HTTPS://DOI.ORG/10.5117/YCBI2024.004.DILL

Child Theology, Spirituality and Intersectionality

Annemie Dillen, KU Leuven[1]

Amy Casteel, KU Leuven

Abstract

Various authors have written on children's spirituality and how spirituality of children can be nurtured. These reflections are mostly inspired by a clear view on children's agency and an emancipatory form of child theology. In this chapter we discuss the question how discrimination on the basis of race, class, and gender can be avoided in initiatives to nurture children's spirituality. What can a feminist postcolonial theology offer in the reflection on religious education and various approaches of nurturing children's spirituality? We discuss the idea of the "oppression olympics," where experiences of being oppressed as a child (in the context of adultism), as a girl or boy (sexism), as someone with less privileges in terms of financial support (classism) or as someone from another ethnicity (racism) are considered as competing each other? How can "child theology" include attention for other perspectives, without falling in the trap of strong "identity politics"? These questions are discussed in dialogue with a contextual and anti-essentialist reading of Mark 10:15.

Keywords: Children, spirituality, intersectionality, social class, bible

1 Our thanks goes to prof. Karen Marie Yust and her colleagues who organized an expert meeting in January 2024 on children's spirituality in Richmond, Virginia (Union Presbyterian Seminary), in the context of the project Real kids, real faith. See https://www.realkidsrealfaith.org. Special thanks goes to the participants of the meeting, who shared their insights, which inspired this chapter.

Mark 10:13–16
People were bringing little children to Jesus for him to place his hands on them, but the disciples rebuked them. When Jesus saw this, he was indignant. He said to them, "Let the little children come to me, and do not hinder them, for the kingdom of God belongs to such as these. Truly I tell you, anyone who will not receive the kingdom of God like a little child will never enter it." And he took the children in his arms, placed his hands on them and blessed them.
(New Revised Standard Version Catholic Edition)

Let the Little Children Come to Me

One of the most cited biblical texts in reference to children is Mark 10:13–16. People want to bring children to Jesus, but his disciples try to prevent this. At that moment, three things happen: 1. Jesus is indignant; 2. Jesus makes a clear verbal statement; 3. Jesus performs a symbolic gesture, by taking the children in his arms and blessing them. Many children's bibles have idyllic pictures of Jesus with the children. Within the Belgian catholic context this text is used in liturgies for first communion and baptism. Each time the idea behind it is: "Jesus is a friend for children." Still, this text has many more meanings, and in the context of reflections on theology about children and theology or spirituality of children, a more social and contextual interpretation of the text might challenge the actual state of the art on theology and children.[2]

Images of Children

In contemporary European and North-American contexts, children are often presented as exceedingly precious. Most parents do not have many children and so parental and societal investment in children is usually quite large. This does not prevent that the phenomenon of adultism is also omnipresent. Adultism means that adults are given a preferential treatment and that children experience unjust discrimination. This can be seen in the presumption that children are not able to contribute to adults meaningfully as knowers of knowledge, formulators of suggestions, or caregivers of others. In other contexts, one can speak about adult centrism, where the norm of

2 See Dillen, "Children."

institutions and societal behaviour are adults. These phenomena can be discovered, for instance, in the tendency to organize flights, restaurants, and hotels "for adults only," but it is also present in more subtle forms, where urban design or general habits and ways of speaking show adult centric biases.

Some contemporary readers might interpret Jesus' words "let the little children come to me" as a prophetic criticism in this context. But the danger of over-idealization of children, based on the biblical words or on parallel societal evolutions, to put children on a pedestal and to foster them as cute, innocent, and vulnerable persons, exists as well. It is important to warn against idealization and essentialization of children. Children are different from each other and although for strategic reasons it is sometimes important to advocate for the interests of children as a group,[3] their experiences, context and personalities are nevertheless very diverse. In this context it is also important to notice that Jesus' words on the example of children and his admonishment to "receive the kingdom of God like a little child" do not have to be considered as an idealization of children's faith and openness. Within the context of studies on children's spirituality, this is an ongoing challenge to be taken into account.

Contextual Readings

Within the context of theology about children and reflections on children's spirituality, it is the US-based practical theologian Joyce Mercer who explains clearly how the biblical text of Mark 10:13–16 should not be read as a form of idealization of children, or as a tribute to the virtue of obedience, and discusses similar ideas about openness, receiving from God and so on. Mercer explains, in reference to biblical scholars, how the context of the biblical texts helps us to see that the children who are brought to Jesus are most likely children of the street; they were not brought to him by their parents, as it is sometimes shown in children's bibles, but they were considered as outcasts, due to their lower social class.[4] One could read the text with the perspective of "class differences" and discrimination of persons living in poverty, rather than limiting it to the adult-child difference.

This interpretation is valuable for at least three reasons. First of all, it adds the aspect of class, and issues on poverty and discrimination, to the

3 See Landry and Maclean, eds., *Spivak*.

4 See Mercer, *Welcoming*, 52.

interpretation of this texts. Put another way, it helps us to read the text from an intersectional perspective, where not only one axis of power is at stake, but the intersection of various axes. Here, at least one axis, the difference between adults and children, intersects with another axis, the difference between persons with social privilege and those without, trying to survive on the streets and to care for themselves.

Children without social privilege tend to be invisible, or rather, made invisible.[5] Of course, in lived experience there is a range within social privilege: it is not typically all or none. The advantages that social privilege bring offer access—the primary theme in the Mark passage. Participating in a flourishing spiritual life through access to God that is unobstructed is a support for children whose social privileges are otherwise limited.[6]

A second reason why this broadening of possible interpretations is relevant refers to the image of children. It not only adds the extra aspect of class, but it also diminishes the strong focus on possible idealizations of children and helps people to see children more from a realistic point of view, showing that there are many differences among children as well. In general, children are not "pure", "innocent", and "examples of faith." Illustrations in children's bibles tend to portray children as still, clean, orderly and attentive. These images codify social preferences which are presented as normative, even as religious ideals. It wouldn't do justice to children to approach them holding such expectations. Taking the differences, the competences, and the struggles of children seriously, also in the context of churches and faith communications, might be more helpful for children than idealized expectations.

A third reason why the interpretation in line with class differences is relevant is partly influenced by the contemporary context from which we write: the Catholic church in Belgium is highly contested because of forms of sexual abuse of minors that were not always taken seriously by the church. One could argue that the text of Mark 10:13–16 and its interpretation that it primarily shows how important children are, should function exactly as a warning against child abuse. However, this straightforward logic has its flipside. Focusing on children and their openness for the kingdom of God bears the risk of putting too much emphasis on the passivity of children and the power difference with adults. An idealized image of children in terms of "openness" might contribute to legitimations of hierarchical power, which could function as a climate for power abuse. There is no automatic

5 See Botha, Yates, and Kotzé, "Children's narrative identity."

6 See Casteel, *Pillars*.

link between all these aspects, but if we want to develop a theology with all the victims or survivors of child sexual abuse in mind, then we have to be careful and warn for possible pitfalls. The text of Mark 10:13–16 is relevant in the context of prevention of abuse as it shows the value of children, especially those who are sometimes neglected and might live in very difficult circumstances. However, if the text leads to a focus on "openness" of children, which sometimes fosters associations of obedience, dependency, and hierarchical differences with adults, one has to speak up and make clear that these interpretations have functioned in the past as legitimations for staying silent when abuse happened. Based on research on bystanders and sexual abuse in the church, it is clear that many bystanders did not take action against the forms of abuse based on ideas such as "they were only children" or "adults know and do what is best for children" and "children have to obey the adults." It is important to recognize the ambivalent use of many texts, and to search for interpretations that help people thrive and stimulate the common good.

Children as Victims and Agents: Beyond the 'Oppression Olympics'?

The addition of the lens of "class" to the interpretation of the text of Mark 10:13–16 is clearly relevant, as shown above, but it also raises at least two new questions.

First, the interpretation that the children who could come to Jesus were those who encountered all forms of exclusion in their daily life, is very valuable, but puts the focus on children as possible victims. Children are vulnerable and have to be cared for. This is a very valuable approach, but this "caretakers" perspective has been complemented in literature by a "child-liberators" perspective, focusing more on children's agency and their rights of participation.[7] Children have their own voice and should not only be protected, but should receive the possibility to contribute to the common good. Their "giving" in general should be seen, as children are human persons and thus subjects whose agency needs attention. This view on children has been developed strongly at the end of the twentieth century, with the publication of the UN Convention on the Rights of the Child in 1989 and the development of what is called "childhood studies."

7 See Dillen, "The Child," 93; Dillen and Gärtner, *Discovering*.

The recent research of Joyce Mercer helps us to see what this agency of children means in concrete contexts.[8] She is one of the scholars who study the meaning of children and young people as prophets arguing for more ecological justice, and warning about climate change. Young persons have been organizing climate strikes, not going to school and demonstrating for more ecological awareness and justice.

A second question comes up in this context, which I learned from Joyce Mercer herself. The focus on climate change and the prophetic actions of young persons might shift the attention to more privileged children and young persons. For many other children, climate justice is a luxury, they would say, as their main struggles centre around poverty, racism, or abuse. This kind of criticism falls under the term "oppression olympics."[9] This term refers to the intellectual debate about which form of oppression deserves most attention. Within my Belgian context, critical questions are raised about the relevance of attention to gender and LGBTQ+ issues, with some political parties stating that these questions take away attention from what really matters for young people, especially those living in underprivileged contexts, such as poverty and lack of proper education or hope for future work. The counter-reaction explains that one focus does not have to exclude the other focus.

Another example, referring to the Belgian context, is the discussion about "black Pete," a figure that is considered to be the assistant of Saint Nicolas, who brings presents to children each year on 6 December. The Pete-figure has colonial roots, and lots of anti-racist protest has asked for rethinking the presentation and the role of this figure.[10] Counterarguments raised in favour of maintaining the situation as it is in many places focus on the relevance of the celebration for children. "Don't take this celebration away from our children," people would say, and argue that the figures should not change. This discussion can be interpreted as a form of "oppression olympics" as well: there seems to be a competition between acting in favour of the children and acting in favour of all persons by condemning a form of racism. However, this competition is often only seen on a discursive level. It is not at all clear that arguing for a different way of celebrating the feast of Saint Nicolas means going against children's interests, especially as many children are nowadays aware of the problems related to colonial images.

8 See Mercer, "Children and Climate Anxiety"; Mercer, "What Children Know."

9 See Hancock, *Solidarity*.

10 See Gruber, "The 'Zwarte Piet' Debate."

Coming back to the arguments about children as prophets for climate justice, this would mean that paying attention to climate justice does not prevent attention to justice in terms of avoiding unjust discrimination based on race, class or gender. The idea that there is an "oppression olympics" is true when one speaks about intellectual debates, but in practice, focusing on more justice in one area contributes to more justice in other areas or, at least, does not make doing so impossible. Climate justice is relevant for everyone, notably for those living in poverty. This is only one example that shows us again the relevance of an intersectional approach, looking at various axes of power at the same time without considering one as more important than, or as threatening to, the other. However, as classical interpretations of intersectionality focus usually on two or more forms of oppression, or a double or triple victimization, we do want to include the relevance of adding the perspectives of agency, prophetic protest, and participation to the approach of multiple forms of discrimination. Children are not only victimized because they are children (and not adults), but also because they might be living in poverty or have a different colour of skin than others, or because they have a gender that is considered as less valuable in their context. At the same time, they might be protesting against some of these or other forms of exclusion, or they might be contributing to society in multiple different ways.

The next question is what this means for contemporary research on children's spirituality.

Intersectionality and Children's Spirituality

Awareness of the complex interwovenness of activity (agency, children as subjects, participants, etc.) and passivity (vulnerability, victimhood, obedience, etc.) is very important, as well as the various axes of social identity on which discrimination and protest against it are happening (age, gender, class, race, etc.). This is a discourse that is based on contemporary insights in feminist and postcolonial studies, as well as within the field of practical theology. One could ask whether such critical awareness of these many layers and complex interweaving of forms of discrimination and protest matters for studies and practices on children's spirituality. The potential for harm from discrimination at these axes is illustrated by Jozine Botha, Hannalie Yates, and Manitza Kotzé, who point out that attitudes and structures that perpetuate the idea "that children lack full rationality, wisdom, and the ability to discern their best interests" can not only inhibit children but can lead to abuse.[11] Whereas the discourse on children's spirituality is very much focused on the axis "children-adults," one could argue for more attention on intersectionality and the relevance of other axes as well. Some examples will illustrate this.

Although it is very difficult for girls to be accepted in many parts of the world or even to get access to education at all, in my own Belgian context, educational systems and forms of religious education in parishes (often called "catechesis") have an implicit bias in favour of girls.[12] Boys are often considered as active, noisy, or paying less attention. Taking inspiration from Jesus, who taught his disciples in both words and actions,[13] it is valuable to consider how to involve children in multiple ways. The opportunity to engage with materiality during catechetical programs addresses the need to regard the entirety of the human being, which is an embodied experience. When parishes reflect on catechetical programs, they could think not only about how to involve children and give them a voice, but also how they could make their catechetical programs attractive for both girls and boys—keeping in mind that the internal differences within these groups are very large. One example could be to provide an educational style with lots of activity, thus avoiding expectations that are not realistic for a large group of children.

Another example of the relevance of intersectional thinking in contexts of nurturing children's spirituality concerns the intersection between children and forms of racism. In religious education classes, handbooks, and pedagogical guidelines, the main focus is often on the question of what is appropriate for children at their age. In the Belgian context, general ideas about avoiding discrimination are common in the context of religious education, but profound attention to white privilege is rather absent. If children hear that the class teacher (who also teaches religious education in the school and is a volunteer catechist in the local parish) uses the n-word to speak about children from a country in Africa, even when a boy from Ghana is present in the class, it is clear that the theme of daily racism and white privilege might be present in some children's minds in this context, but clearly not in the teacher's behaviour. Speech acts like this reveal a deeper need for critiquing whiteness as a norm within Christianity and in the broader community. At the same time, since the static representations of race in literature appear to be permanent, they both reinforce and justify the verbal

11 See Botha, Yates, and Kotzé, "Children's narrative identity."

12 See Van de Gaer, De Munter, and Van Damme, "Effecten."

13 See Csinos, "Come."

and structural assertions that contribute to maintaining racial hierarchy.[14] Given this sense of permanence, perhaps addressing the materials offers an opportunity to also address the practices and underlying assumptions. Materials used in catechetical settings, in parish communications (e.g., websites, pictures) could be screened not only in terms of their aptness for children and children from various family backgrounds, but also in terms of ethnic diversity. Do these materials present diversity and do they make it possible that children of all backgrounds feel welcome?

A third example of the relation between (nurturing) children's spirituality on the one hand and various aspects of social identity on the other hand relates to poverty and social class. Groups of children are welcomed in parishes, not only during liturgical celebrations referring to Mark 10:13–16. And it is precisely these moments when attention may be focused on children as still, clean, orderly, and attentive as portrayed in those illustrations, or as performers who entertain and bring hope to adults. However, is there enough attention for those who do not have the privilege to pay for catechesis lessons? Which examples are used in liturgy and catechesis when people teach—do their examples refer to privileged contexts (with, e.g, safe caregivers, comfortable housing, holidays abroad, and time for bringing their children to special activities)? Or are persons nurturing children's spirituality aware of the diversity in background and experiences of the children they are working with?

It is important that children not only learn about faith and what spirituality might mean for them personally, it is also very relevant that they are seen, along with their individual backgrounds. Children have to receive recognition for who they are, which means it is important that they are not subjected to the (implicit and often unconscious) message that they do not belong in a particular group.

More research on the intersection between children's spirituality and various forms of exclusion or discrimination is needed, as well as research on children's own contributions, their voice in terms of spirituality, and in terms of acting as an "upstander" (an active bystander) or someone who protests against forms of discrimination.

14 See Cressler, "Centering."

Conclusion

In this chapter, we added an extra layer to the general discourse on children, theology, and children's spirituality. Various authors have written on children's spirituality and how it can be nurtured. These reflections are mostly inspired by a clear view on children's agency and an emancipatory form of child theology. One of the recent questions is how can discrimination on the basis of race, class, and gender be avoided in initiatives to nurture children's spirituality? We explained how there is a discourse on the "oppression olympics," where experiences of being oppressed as a child (in the context of adultism), as a girl or boy (sexism), as someone with fewer privileges, e.g., in terms of financial support (classism) or as someone from another ethnicity (racism) are competing against each other. This competition should be reduced to a way of analysing arguments and counterarguments, but does not necessarily let itself be found in reality, where the complexity and intersectionality of various axes is omnipresent. A contextual and anti-essentialist reading of Mark 10:15 helps to illustrate that taking care of children and taking care of people living in poverty might go together, also in the interpretation of the text. It also shows that essentialization and romanticization of children should be avoided. As such, this chapter offers various stimuli to take children seriously as they are, in all their diversity. It might be difficult to take care of all aspects at the same time, and to fight against all forms of oppression at the same moment. Also there, Mark 10:13–16 might offer help. The focus on children's openness for the kingdom of God is not unambivalent, as we have made clear in this text. However, it is acceptable to interpret this as an admonishment to combat all forms of "manufacturability." Human beings cannot create everything, and perfection is not feasible. The text of Mark 10:13–16 also stimulates the eschatological belief in God who might complete all work of human persons that stays unaccomplished, imperfect, and ambivalent. Or, in other words, the fear of not being able to be perfect in light of all the complexities we have sketched above, does not have to prevent human action supported by a belief in God and eschatological promises.

Bibliography

Botha, Jozine G., Hannelie Yates, Manitza Kotzé. "Children's narrative identity formation. Towards a childist narrative theology of praxis." *HTS Teologiese Studies* 80:1 (2024): 1–9. https://doi.org/10.4102/hts.v80i1.9575.

Casteel, Amy. "Pillars of Salt. Pastoral Care with Adolescents with a Migration Experience." *Religions* 13:2 (2022): 184. https://doi.org/10.3390/rel13020184.

Cressler, Matthew J. "Centering Black Catholic Religio-Racial Identity, Revealing White Catholicism." *Journal of the American Academy of Religion* 88:2 (2020): 304–28. https://doi.org/10.1093/jaarel/lfaa013.

Csinos, David M., "'Come, Follow Me'. Apprenticeship in Jesus' Approach to Education." *Religious Education* 105:1 (2010): 45–62. doi:10.1080/00344080903472725.

Dillen, Annemie. "Children and Christian Theology." In *St Andrews Encyclopaedia of Theology*, edited by B. N. Wolfe et al, 2024. Accessed November 18, 2024. https://www.saet.ac.uk/Christianity/ChildrenandChristianTheology.

Dillen, Annemie. "The Child 'as a Child'. A Theological-Ethical Investigation of the Concrete and Relational Giving of a Child." In *The Given Child. The Religions' Contribution to Children's Citizenship*, edited by T. Wyller and U. Nayar. Göttingen: Vandenhoeck & Ruprecht, 2007, 83–103.

Dillen, Annemie, and Stefan Gärtner. *Discovering Practical Theology. Exploring Boundaries*. Leuven: Peeters, 2020.

Gruber, Judith. "The 'Zwarte Piet' Debate in Belgium and the Netherlands – Searching for Racial Reconciliation in Post/colonial Europe? Theologizing about Social Conflict and Cohesion at the Intersection of Race and Religion." *Louvain Studies* 45:1 (2022): 34–59.

Hancock, Ange-Marie. *Solidarity Politics for Millennials. A Guide to Ending the Oppression Olympics*. New York: Palgrave Macmillan, 2001.

Landry, Donna, and Gerald MacLean, eds. *The Spivak Reader. Selected works of Gayatri Chakravorty Spivak*. London: Routledge, 1996.

Mercer, Joyce Ann. *Welcoming Children. A Practical Theology of Childhood*. St. Louis: Chalice Press, 2005.

Mercer, Joyce Ann. "Children and Climate Anxiety. An Ecofeminist Practical Theological Perspective." *Religions* 13:4 (2022): 302. https://doi.org/10.3390/rel13040302.

Mercer, Joyce Ann. "What Children Know. Children, Climate Change, and Epistemic Injustice." *Pastoral Psychology* (2024). https://doi.org/10.1007/s11089-024-01146-7.

Van de Gaer, Eva, Agnes De Munter and Jan van Damme. "Effecten van individuele attitudes en van de attitudes van de peergroup op de prestaties voor wiskunde van jongens en meisjes." *Pedagogiek* 24:1 (2004): 23–40.

Amsterdam University Press

YEARBOOK OF CONTEXTUAL BIBLICAL INTERPRETATION 1 (2024) 57-76
HTTPS://DOI.ORG/10.5117/YCBI2024.005.KUMM

What Hope for Children? Eschatology, the Normativity of the Future, and Christian Hope in Godly Play

Armin M. Kummer, KU Leuven, Faculty of Theology and Religious Studies, Research Unit of Pastoral and Empirical Theology, arminmanuel.kummer@kuleuven.be

Abstract

What role does Christian hope play in the contextual biblical interpretation with children? This chapter examines the core teaching materials of the Godly Play method with regards to their treatment of the future. The analysis uncovers a preponderance of backward-looking narratives at the expense of future-oriented perspectives. While Godly Play aims to instill a "playful orthodoxy" and prepare children for church liturgy, the analysis leads to the conclusion that it suffers from an eschatological deficit, a neglect of Christian hope. In the light of these findings, the chapter argues for a shift in Godly-Play's narrative and interactive methodology and underscores the imperative of integrating the Bieringer school's *Normativity of the Future* approach to biblical hermeneutics into the Godly Play religious-education practices. It encourages Godly-Play storytellers to reevaluate and enrich their pedagogical approach to reflect the profound importance of Christian eschatology and hope for children's theology and spirituality.

Keywords: Godly Play, contextual biblical interpretation, biblical hermeneutics, hope, eschatology, religious education, mystagogical catechesis, ritual.

Wondering, Godly-Play Style

I wonder…
I wonder what the future will be like…
I wonder: how will it be, when all of God's promises finally come true.
I wonder: what do we know about God's future?
I wonder: what does it look like, our Christian hope?
There is a sentence in 1 Peter 3:15:
"Always be ready to give an answer to everyone who asks you to give an account of the hope that is in you".
I wonder: am I ready to answer everyone who asks me?
I wonder: what account of our hope can I give?
In the shadow of war, genocide, disease, and famine, in the shadow of climate change and ecological degradation: what answers are we ready to give?
And I wonder: who will ask us to give such an account?
I wonder, why would they ask us?
I wonder, do we look more hopeful than others?

Introduction

This chapter wonders which narrative accounts are given in religious education for "the hope that is in us"? What place, in more technical terms, does eschatology find in contextual biblical interpretation with children? What place, to narrow it down to a precise research question, does the future have in Godly Play, a popular method of biblical didactics?

This chapter starts with a brief theological perspective on Christian hope. Rather than providing a rough outline of biblical eschatology, which would be futile given the limitations of this article, it will very briefly introduce the *Normativity of the Future* approach, developed by Leuven exegete Reimund Bieringer and propagated by several of his former students. With its particular take on eschatology, it is a hermeneutical method for biblical texts which operationalizes the theological understanding of hope as an anticipation of God's promised future. Secondly, this chapter will discuss the importance of Christian hope within religious education. Hope, if it constitutes a key ingredient of children's spirituality, helps to foster resilience in the face of global challenges.

In the core analytical part, this chapter examines the core teaching materials of Godly Play with regards to their treatment of the future. The analysis uncovers a strong focus on backward-looking narratives rather than on future-oriented perspectives. While Godly Play aims to instill a "playful orthodoxy" and prepare children for church liturgy, the analysis leads us to conclude that there is a neglect of the eschatological dimension of Christian faith.

In the light of these findings, the final section of the chapter argues for a shift in Godly-Play's narrative and interactive methodology. In its conclusion, this chapter underscores the imperative of integrating the Normativity of the Future approach into religious-education practice. It wants to encourage Godly-Play practitioners to reevaluate and enrich their pedagogical approach to reflect the profound importance of Christian eschatology and hope for children's theology and spirituality.

The Normativity of the Future?

The title of this chapter mentions three key ideas: future, hope, and eschatology. As a first step towards understanding the phenomenon of Christian hope, it is useful to briefly examine these terms.

"Future" is both an everyday word and a grammatical concept in our language. However, within the horizon of the biblical narrative, it has a specifically theological meaning. There is a distinct relationship between the God of the Bible and the future. The God of the biblical narrative is a God of promise. God promises, again and again, a future that is different from the reality experienced in the here and now. There are different names or metaphors for this vision of God's future: for example, the kingdom of God, the city of God, new creation, new Jerusalem, a new heaven and a new earth.

Another word that one tends to use rather carelessly in everyday life is "hope." As a verb, "I hope" is mostly used as a synonym for "I wish." Christian hope, however, has a clearly defined object. Christian hope is the human reaction to God's promises. Christian hope means living towards God's promised future. When Christians hope, they make God's future already an effective force that can be experienced in the present.

The third term, "eschatology," is far removed from everyday speech and hardly used outside expert theological circles. It is a term used in systematic theology and refers to a systematic subdiscipline that theologizes about our hoping. Eschatology speculates about how God's future will be different from the present we experience today.

The German systematic theologian, Jürgen Moltmann, deplored in 1964 that eschatology had become a mere annex to systematic theology, something quite peripheral to what most Christians believed. Officially, eschatological doctrines about Christ's return, judgment, the resurrection of the dead, and eternal life are in fact confessed every Sunday in the Creed. Otherwise, they do not receive much attention, neither in church life nor in theology, and certainly not in religious education.

Against this widespread neglect of eschatology, Moltmann argues that

> Christianity is eschatology in its entirety and not just in the appendix, it is hope, a prospect and orientation towards the future, and therefore also a departure and transformation of the present. The eschatological is not something about Christianity, it is in fact the medium of the Christian faith, the tone to which everything in it is tuned, the colour of the dawn of an expected new day, in which everything here is immersed.[1]

The most central topic of Christian theology, according to Moltmann, is the future. God is the God of the future. Especially the Exodus narrative and the texts of the biblical prophets depict God as the one who meets his people in God's promised future.[2] Importantly, for Moltmann, this future orientation is by no means understood to serve as a sedative or as cheap comfort. It is not meant to be what Karl Marx called "opium for the people," something that numbs the senses and distracts people's attention away from the challenges of the present. On the contrary, Christian hoping for God's future makes believers critical of, and often opposed to, the reality that we find in the present world of suffering, evil, and death. Christian hope instils a restless longing and stimulates believers to change the world. Hope in God's future is a driving force of social transformation.[3]

Flemish practical theologian Annemie Dillen also emphasizes the "inseparable linkage" between Christian existence and hope. In her discussion of hope, she enters into critical dialogue with various disciplines (esp. psychology) and their views of hope (a trait of attitude). Dillen recognizes the importance of Moltmann and deplores that "his theology has long remained unexplored in dialogue with pastoral practices."[4]

Biblical exegete Reimund Bieringer has elaborated a hermeneutic approach which he calls the *Normativity of the Future*.[5] His quest touched on

1 Moltmann, *Hoffnung*, 12. Own translation.

2 See Moltmann, *Hoffnung*, 127.

3 See Moltmann, *Hoffnung*, 304–12.

4 Dillen, "Hope."

5 See Elsbernd and Bieringer, *When Love Is Not Enough*; Bieringer and Elsbernd, "Interpreting the Signs"; Bieringer and Elsbernd, "The 'Normativity of the Future' Approach"; Bieringer, "Texts That Create a Future"; Bieringer, "The Normativity of the Future."

fundamental theology as he sought to identify "the locus of authority in our revelatory texts."[6] Bieringer based his approach on the hermeneutic theories of Hans Gadamer, Paul Ricoeur, and Sarah Schneiders on the one hand, and on Vatican II's theology of revelation on the other.[7] For Bieringer, the alternative world projected by a biblical text becomes "the real referent of the text, the truth claim of the text"[8] and thus the locus of revelation. Later, Bieringer extended the *Normativity of the Future* approach into a general hermeneutical approach that is no longer limited to the interpretation of texts, but of life itself.[9] The meaning of "future" has evolved from literary projection to a theological understanding of "the eschatological in-breaking of the future into the present."[10] In this later conception of the *Normativity of the Future* approach, texts no longer merely project their own futures, but "create conditions of possibility for the in-breaking of the vision of an alternative world, a just and inclusive community."[11] Bieringer argues that the *Normativity of the Future* approach can be employed as an " approach to life itself".[12] For him, the future enjoys a "*hermeneutic privilege* over the past and the present."[13]

In some of my own prior work, I have offered some critical reflections on the *Normativity of the Future* approach, and ventured to claim that, for Christians, a hermeneutics of hope, an orientation towards the future, is indeed strongly supported by the Christian tradition. This claim can be supported with a philosophical and a theological argument.[14]

The Philosophical Argument

We experience human life as a journey through time. The human person is a historical being, or, vice versa, history is constitutive of the human condition. It is therefore indispensable for the self-constitution of human identity to define the way one relates to history. In public discourse, and especially pronounced in political discourse, I always find two fundamental

6 Bieringer and Elsbernd, "Interpreting the Signs," 50.
7 Bieringer, "Biblical Revelation"; Bieringer, "Dialogical Revelation?"
8 Bieringer, "The Normativity of the Future," 42.
9 Bieringer and Elsbernd, "The 'Normativity of the Future' Approach," 8.
10 Bieringer and Elsbernd, "The 'Normativity of the Future' Approach," 9.
11 Bieringer and Elsbernd, "The 'Normativity of the Future' Approach," 10.
12 Bieringer and Elsbernd, "The 'Normativity of the Future' Approach," 8.
13 Bieringer and Elsbernd, "The 'Normativity of the Future' Approach," 12. Italics in the original.
14 The following two arguments have been previously published in Kummer, *Men*, 78–82.

options for relating to history. One can either move towards the future or try to re-live the past. Accordingly, personal and social motivations are located either in the past or in the future. A hopeful orientation, directed towards the future, is often associated with sociopolitical progressivism. A nostalgic orientation, directed towards the past, is frequently associated with sociopolitical conservatism.

One can easily recognize backward-looking discourse in political slogans that contain words like "back" and "again", as in "Make America great *again*,"[15] or "I want my country *back*."[16] What these slogans have in common is a linear view of history, where the past is always superior to the present. History presents itself in this view as a slippery downward slope, a continuous deterioration and ever-increasing alienation from a fictitious golden past. Here, normativity rests in this past. The future, as far as it entails change and differs from the idealized past, is best to be avoided. The ethical implication of this downward trajectory is to stop historical progress and, ideally, to travel back in time.[17]

In contrast, a forward-looking perspective is directed towards the future and embraces newness and change. In this view, the future is nothing to be afraid of. Instead, it inspires hope and creative imagination. The course of history holds the promise of improvement, a steady upward movement. Normativity rests not so much in an ideologically constructed fiction of what has been, but in the open-ended potentialities of dreams and visions. The ethical impulse of this future-oriented outlook is to move forward.

In the sphere of public discourse, many political debates are framed within this binary. Political discourse often seems to suggest that there was an actual choice between going forward and going back, between accepting historical change and turning the clock back Yet are these two alternatives really equally viable options? Is it, after all, possible to turn the clock back and to relive the past? Heraclitus rightly observed "πάντα ῥεῖ" (everything flows) and he therefore maintained that "you cannot step

15 U.S. Republican Presidential candidate Donald Trump during the U.S. Presidential campaigns 2016 and 2024.

16 British opposition politician Nigel Farage during the Brexit referendum, 2016.

17 This kind of nostalgia is not limited to the political sphere. It can often be encountered among erudite lovers of art and culture, who hold that cultural achievements have peaked at some point (e.g., in Bach's music, Shakespeare's drama or seventeenth century Dutch painting) and civilization has been on a downhill ride ever since. Woody Allen depicts this worldview beautifully in his 2011 movie "Midnight in Paris." Two great proponents of such cultural pessimism were Spengler, *Der Untergang*; and, more recently, Bloom, *The Western Canon*.

into the same stream twice."[18] Given the flow of history, the inescapability of historical change, turning back the clock simply is not a viable option. To resist history's pull towards the future is an absurd proposition and ultimately amounts to a form of nihilism. This is the philosophical case against backward-oriented worldviews.

The Biblical Tradition

There is also a biblical-theological case to be made in favour of a future-orientation. Nostalgia, one could argue, finds no support in the scriptures of the Jewish and Christian traditions. The past is never portrayed as normative. Normativity is always located in the future.

When God calls human beings in the Hebrew Bible narratives, there is always a forward movement towards a better place. When God calls Abram, his ancestor's home in Haran is not presented as the normative place for human flourishing. When God calls Israel out of Egypt, the Exodus is a journey towards a better future. As a matter of fact, the Exodus narrative does not deny the possibility of nostalgia. In the wilderness, the Israelites start complaining, longing to go back to the fleshpots of Egypt.[19] Yet the narrative never endorses such nostalgia.

The key biblical narrative about looking back is the story of Lot's wife. Lot and his family are the only ones to be saved from the destruction of Sodom, and they are warned not to look back. Lot's wife is unable to suppress her nostalgic and backward-looking instincts, and turns into a pillar of salt, which I would like to consider a powerful metaphor of the calcifying, life-denying results of conservative nihilism.

In the Prophets, the ethical message is never one of returning to the superior life of a golden past. The prophetic call is always a call towards an alternative future. Even the exile experience, while it can be framed in terms of the tearful memory of a place, never amounts to a nostalgic longing for the past. The theological message (in the OT) that God acts in and through history towards a better future rules out the option of ever turning back the clock.

The New Testament projects its own hermeneutics of hope. In the gospels, there is not a single instance where Jesus pines for the past. In Luke 17:32, Jesus uses the example of Lot's wife as a warning to his disciples. Jesus'

18 See Crescenzo, *Geschichte*, 85.

19 See Ex. 16:3 (KJV, NRSV).

proclamation is all about the in-breaking future, the reign of God, the eschatological gift of the Spirit. Jesus' parables are about progress—often couched in agricultural images of slow but certain growth. The Johannine Jesus encouragingly points his followers to a future that surpasses the present of his earthly life—"they will do even greater things than I have done."[20]

Paul, in his letters, looks back at his own past—and considers it rubbish.[21] The past is no longer normative for him. For him, the Spirit-filled future shapes the life and worldview of God's children.[22]

Placing the locus of normativity in the future does not imply that the past should not be treasured.[23] Memory is not the same as nostalgia. The narrative traditions of the Hebrew Bible are witness to Israel's collective memory. Walter Brueggemann claims that "Israel characteristically retold all of its experience through the powerful, definitional lens of the Exodus memory."[24] Right up to today, Jews celebrate Exodus memory annually with the Passover festival. But the Passover does not commemorate a golden past that anyone would like to go back to. The central event of the festival is the *Haggadah*, the family ceremony that culminates in the hopeful pledge "Next Year in Jerusalem!"[25] This is hardly an expression of nostalgia. The celebration of Exodus memory serves as an expression of collective hope in a better future. The point of biblical memory is to give historical depth to our hope.[26]

Christian Hope in Religious Education

In the wake of Moltmann and Bieringer, the previous section developed an argument for the centrality and normativity of the future for Christian worldview and practice. What does this imply for religious education?

A number of theologians in the field of religious education clearly endorse the emphasis on Christian hope. In his textbook on biblical didactics, Ingo

20 Καὶ μείζονα τούτων ποιήσει. John 14:12.

21 Phil. 3:8 (NRSV)

22 See, e.g., Rom. 8; Gal. 3:26–4:7.

23 On Christian spirituality and present-moment awareness, see Kummer, "You Shall Love YHWH", 42–43.

24 Brueggemann, *Theology*, 177.

25 See Hoffman, "Haggadah of Pessah"; Walfish, "Pesah"; Robinson, *Essential Judaism*, 118–26.

26 This is also how I understand J.B. Metz's notion of "dangerous memory": "It is precisely because Christians believe in an eschatological meaning for history that they can risk historical consciousness." See Metz, *A Passion*, 40.

Baldermann goes even so far as to claim that hope is the single comprehensive theme of the entire Bible.[27] Theology, he claims, is there to help people learn to fight the battle with despair. This requires a didactic approach that enables each and every believer to confront despair.[28] "Under all conditions and circumstances, [...] a responsible pedagogy today must see to it that it enables students to grasp something like a sustainable hope on their own."[29] Very much in the tradition of Moltmann, Baldermann points out:

> Hope is only sustainable if it does not speak of a turning point that will arrive sometime in the future, but shows ways of how to do something hopeful now and to live in the spirit of this hope.[30]

In his 2016 Presidential Address to the *Religious Education Association* in Pittsburgh, Bert Roebben of Bonn University asserts that generating hope is the primary task of the teaching profession.[31] Along very similar lines, Mary Elizabeth Moore of Boston University claims that "the measure of our teaching is the degree to which our message and manner conform to the love of God and participate in hope for a transformed world."[32]

Hope and Future in Godly Play

In the light of the previous sections, it should be clear that, and hope and future-orientation must be considered of theological importance, and why. This raises the question whether and how Christian hope can be a topic in the context of Religious Education. The remainder of this chapter looks more closely into how children and young people encounter hope and future-orientation in the context of Godly Play sessions.

27 See Baldermann, *Einführung*, 11.
28 See Baldermann, *Einführung*, 6.
29 Baldermann, *Einführung*, 14. Own translation.
30 Baldermann, *Einführung*, 10. Own translation.
31 Roebben, "Generating Hope."
32 Moore, "Teaching," 78.

Personal Remarks

Late modern hermeneutics no longer pretends to approach its subject from a neutral or objective standpoint.[33] Recognizing that our horizons are shaped by our traditions and our personal pre-commitments,[34] it requires the self-disclosure of the researcher's own personal context and positionality. Before approaching my research object, the Godly Play method, I therefore need to provide some information about my own personal history with Godly Play.

I first encountered Godly Play in February 2015, at the Child Theology Conference hosted by the Faculty of Theology and Religious Studies of KU Leuven.[35] Conference participants were invited to take part in several Godly Play sessions. I immediately found this immersive and experiential method of biblical didactics immensely attractive. I have since been trained as a Godly Play storyteller, and, as a member of the church council of a large international congregation in Brussels, where I was in charge of the children and youth ministry. I started a process which resulted in many of our volunteers received training as Godly Play storytellers. Godly Play, which requires significant investments in training and material, became a central element of Sunday School ministry. I have also used the Godly Play method in classes I taught as a religious-education teacher at the International German School in Brussels. Furthermore, I have used Godly Play elements in the context of my pastoral work with professional men. On the scholarly side, I co-published an article with Jeroen Hendrickx and Annemie Dillen on the use of the Godly-Play method in Flemish schools.[36] Finally, Godly Play has had an important impact on my preaching style. I gave a sample of this in the introductory sequence of this chapter. I find it helpful to approach Scripture with "wondering questions".[37] I do not think it should be the job of a preacher or instructor to proclaim the "correct" interpretation of a biblical text. I believe that the best homilies are those which invite each member of the audience to approach the interpretation of biblical texts with contextual "wondering questions." To wonder "what part of the story is the most important," "what part of the story is about you," and "what part of the story we could leave out."[38] These are excellent questions. Once you start

33 See, e.g., Bordo, *The Flight.*

34 See Gadamer, *Wahrheit und Methode.*

35 "Trusting Children and God: Religiosity in Early Childhood," Network Conference on Child Theology. Leuven: February 25-27, 2015.

36 See Hendrickx, Kummer, and Dillen, "Godly Play."

37 Berryman, *Complete Guide 1*, 15f., 56; Berryman, *Teaching*, 45-54.

38 See, e.g., Berryman, *Complete Guide 2*, 71.

asking them, they seem so natural, but I am grateful to Jerome Berryman for formulating and popularizing these questions.

In short, I must declare my positionality as a great fan of Godly Play as an immersive method for biblical didactics and interpretation. The following subsection will show, however, that this does not mean that I am not ready to take a critical stance on what I perceive to be the *lacunae* or *desiderata* in this method.

Analysis: Looking Forward or Backward in Godly Play

The original canon of Jerome Berryman's Godly Play lessons consists of fifty-four lessons for the church year. Fourteen lessons for fall (volume 2),[39] twenty for winter (volume 3),[40] and another twenty for spring (volume 4).[41] Among those fifty-four lessons, a distinction is drawn between twenty-eight "core presentations" (twelve for winter, fifteen for spring and nine for fall) and eighteen "enrichment presentations" (eight for winter, five for spring, and another five for fall). The question motivating this critical analysis is how Godly Play lessons refer to the future.

In storytelling, three time horizons are possible. Storytellers may turn backward and talk about the past, they may talk about the present, or they may turn forward and talk about the future. Usually, the grammatical tense of the verb indicates which of these three options is chosen. In addition, storytellers can do more than just deliver a step-by-step account of past action.[42] They can summarize, interpret, and establish backward and forward links. Importantly, when storytelling presents itself as a performance before an audience, storytellers usually want to establish some explicit links between their story and their audience.

In this light, one can distinguish Godly Play lessons by their time horizons. A first category of lessons tells a story about the past. Even if the audience is invited to imagine "where you are in the story,"[43] the direction of this imaginative time travel is backwards in time. No explicit link is established with the present. A second category of lessons tells a story about the past

39 Berryman, *Complete Guide 2*.

40 Berryman, *Complete Guide 3*, 3.

41 Berryman, *Complete Guide 4*, 4.

42 Obviously, the plot of Godly Play's "sacred stories" is always about the past, be it a fictional or historical past. Some others of the Godly Play lessons are not of a narrative nature, but classified as "Liturgical Actions" or synthesis.

43 See, e.g., Berryman, *Complete Guide 2*, 56.

but establishes a link to the listeners' current reality. In this case, the time horizon of the story reaches from the past up to the present. Finally, a third category of lessons speaks about the future. In this case, the time horizon of the story reaches from a past before the audience's present into the audience's future. These are lessons that make statements about the future.

As a very condensed illustration of these three horizons, one can turn to the "The Flood and the Ark" lesson.[44] The story ends with the animals leaving the ark: "Suddenly all the creatures saw a great bow in the sky. It was a bow of many colors."[45] This is an example of the first option. The audience hears about events in the past.

Then the narrator goes on: "You can still see it today when there is rain and the sun is shining. Today we call it a rainbow."[46] This is an example of the second option. The narrator speaks of the audience's here and now.

Finally, the narrator concludes "This rainbow was God's sign to say that God will never send such a flood again."[47] Here, the narrative builds a connection between past and future. The "never again" can be counted as a statement about the future.

In my analysis, I found that in ten of the fifty-four lessons, the storyteller establishes a link to the audience's present. This is the case with five of the Old Testament lessons, and five of the New Testament stories.

But what about the future? Here one needs to look indeed very closely. Two of the Old Testament stories that were counted among those with a link to the present also contain some form of reference to the future ("The Flood and the Ark" and "The Holy Family"):

In "The Flood and the Ark" the narrator explains, "This rainbow was God's sign to say that God will never send such a flood again."[48] This is a negative statement about the future, but it is clearly forward looking. "Never" refers to a future that is even still a future from the point of view of today's audience.

In the enrichment lesson "Prophets"[49] the narrator concludes, "Prophets come from all kinds of places and are all kinds of people. So some of you in this circle may be or become prophets." Here, "some of you [...] may [...] become" also clearly refers to the current audience's future.

In addition, in the various lessons about Jesus' parables (volume 3, lessons 5–12), the narrator uses a repetitive introductory formula referring to the

44 Berryman, *Complete Guide* 2, 49–56.
45 Berryman, *Complete Guide* 2, 55.
46 Berryman, *Complete Guide* 2, 55.
47 Berryman, *Complete Guide* 2, 56.
48 Berryman, *Complete Guide* 2, 56.
49 Berryman, *Complete Guide* 2, 100–6.

meta-narrative level regarding the parable genre. "If you do not understand the parable today, you may do so in the future." "One day the parable will open up for you."[50] Here, the narrator speaks about the individual listener's future.

Furthermore, in volume 4, there are two "liturgical action" lessons dealing with the Eucharist. They quote Jesus' words of institution, which are forward-looking: in "The Faces of Easter VI," the narrator quotes Jesus, "Whenever you break the bread like this and share it, I will be there," and "Whenever you share a cup of wine like this, I will be there."[51] Likewise, in "The Synagogue and the Upper Room," the narrator quotes Jesus, "When you share the bread like this, I will be there." And "When you share the wine like this, I will be there."[52]

"Circle of the Holy Eucharist" is another non-narrative lesson.[53] It is an explanatory walk through church liturgy. In its summary of the eucharistic prayer, it touches upon the eschaton: "The priest also prays for us to be sanctified, so we will be able to faithfully receive this holy Sacrament and serve God in unity, constancy and peace, and at the last day to join with all the saints in the joy of God's eternal kingdom."[54] This non-biblical text arguably constitutes the most explicitly eschatological statement in all of the Godly Play material.

Finally, the spring series contains one enrichment presentation that is called "The Part That Hasn't Been Written Yet." It is a lesson where the storyteller does not tell a story but encourages the audience to work individually. However, the instruction to the storytellers, although somewhat cryptic, is remarkably future-oriented: "The journey with the elusive presence of God will continue. We are not sure what will happen. The future is the time of the children."[55] However, it is noteworthy that these words are not actually directed to any children, but they are part of the background information in the instructions for the storyteller.

50 Berryman, *Complete Guide 3*, 89, 97, 103, 112, 117.
51 Berryman, *Complete Guide 4*, 61.
52 Berryman, *Complete Guide 4*, 103.
53 Berryman, *Complete Guide 4*, 106–13.
54 Berryman, *Complete Guide 4*, 143.
55 Berryman, *Complete Guide 4*, 143.

In summary, one can identify five different types of future-orientation in the core canon:

1. First, biblical texts where a character from the past speaks about the future in direct speech. We found this in New Testament narratives where Jesus speaks about the future.[56]
2. In a second type, the storyteller interprets or paraphrases something as referring to the future ("This rainbow was God's sign to say that God will never send such a flood again").[57]
3. A third type describes moments when the storyteller talks about the future that lies ahead of the child audience.[58]
4. In a fourth type, the instructor addresses the storyteller with a statement about the children's future.[59]
5. Finally, in a fifth type, the storyteller speaks to the audience about the eschatological future.[60]

If we apply a rather generous measure of future-orientation and include all five types of lessons, we arrive at a total number of eleven future-oriented lessons. If we take narrower criteria and look more specifically for eschatological motives, only "The Flood and the Ark,"[61] "The Faces of Easter VI,"[62] and "The Synagogue and the Upper Room"[63] mention God's promises and Christian hope. What this analysis also reveals, is that at least thirty-five lessons deal neither with the future nor even with the present. They are entirely backward looking.

Discussion

Looking at these results, one can quite objectively say that there is very little future-orientation in the lessons of Godly Play. Whether one refers to it as "Christian hope," "eschatology," or "God's alternative world," the future does not receive much attention in Godly Play.

56 Berryman, *Complete Guide 4*, 61.
57 Berryman, *Complete Guide 2*, 56.
58 Berryman, *Complete Guide 3*, 89, 97, 103, 112, 117.
59 Berryman, *Complete Guide 4*, 143.
60 Berryman, *Complete Guide 4*, 143.
61 Berryman, *Complete Guide 2*, 49–56.
62 Berryman, *Complete Guide 4*, 57–62.
63 Berryman, *Complete Guide 4*, 99–105.

Of course, one can take different positions on whether this matters. It is always somewhat unfair to criticize another author's intellectual creation for what it does not contain. Every author has to make choices about what to concentrate on and what to leave out. Jerome Berryman has always been quite clear about what matters most to him. He wants to introduce children to the "Christian language system," as he calls it. He has declared that his learning outcome is meant to be a "playful orthodoxy." Berryman wants to prepare children for church liturgy, and especially for the eucharist. He speaks of "worship education,"[64] which also includes an appreciation of ecclesial architecture, language, and community. Godly Play prepares children for church membership and participation in the liturgy. Godly Play seeks to preserve and transmit a narrative tradition. Eschatology and hope as engines of social transformation are simply not among Berryman's priorities.[65]

Still, looking at Berryman's Godly-Play materials from a *Normativity of the Future* perspective, one cannot but recognize an eschatological deficit.

Performing the Last Act

The British Dominican theologian and philosopher Herbert McCabe writes:

> There are many groups whose purpose is to ensure that something of the past is made real for the present, (whether it be the Glorious Revolution, the taking of the Bastille, the smashing of the Van); this indeed is the purpose of any group that seeks to preserve the historical identity of a people. Such remembrance is a very large part of the business of education – to recognise and realise our past is to discover ourselves. Now the business of the church is to remember the future. Not merely to remember that there is to be a future, but mysteriously to make the future really present.[66]

McCabe's key point here is to assert the normativity of the future as the core business of Christianity. On the one hand, this means to remember the

64 Berryman, *Godly Play*, 17ff.

65 Berryman's treatment of the Beatitudes is telling. He refers to them as "the true happiness-makers"; see Berryman, *Complete Guide 8*, 47. This reveals an individualistic-therapeutic perspective on what others would consider the most pointed articulation of Jesus social vision of an alternative world. See, e.g., Wengst, *Das Regierungsprogramm*.

66 McCabe, *Law*, 141.

future, and on the other hand, to make it present. Both Reimund Bieringer and the British exegete Nicolas Thomas (N. T. or Tom) Wright describe in similar imagery how the church remembers the future and makes it present.

Bieringer suggests that "the reading community has the task of reading and internalizing the ancient text as the first chapters of a chain novel of which they have to write the next chapter."[67] Elsewhere, he underlines the continued activity of the Holy Spirit in the church: "It inspires people and communities of any age to write their own 'fifth gospel.'"[68]

N. T. Wright proposes in similar fashion to understand the biblical narratives as four acts of a five-act drama. The fifth act is still being written:

> The church would live under the "authority" of the extant story, being required to offer an improvisatory performance of the final act as it leads up to and anticipates the intended conclusion.[69]

This is something the *Normativity of the Future* approach can fruitfully contribute to biblical didactics and, more broadly, to religious education. The challenge for religious education is to do more than just lead children through the museum of church traditions. Instead, it could rather be understood as the playful curatorship of ancient narratives and rituals. The *Normativity of the Future* approach invites children to be not only spectators, but to become the actors in the performance of the final act.

This poses a challenge which the growing community of Godly-Play practitioners, teachers, and scholars need to reflect: How can one re-design Godly-Play lessons in ways that make children the actors in the last act. On the one hand, this challenge raises questions about content: Which additional stories need to be told? On the other hand, it also raises questions about language and perspective: How can Godly-Play storytellers tell sacred stories in words and symbols that "create conditions of possibility for the in-breaking of the vision of an alternative world, a just and inclusive community."[70]

Finally, it is worth highlighting one area that potentially might be particularly fruitful. It is an area where the *Normativity of the Future* approach and Berryman's priorities seem to converge: "the feast."[71] Celebrated with fruit

67 Bieringer, "Texts," 110.

68 Bieringer, "Biblical Revelation," 52.

69 Wright, *New Testament*, 142.

70 Bieringer and Elsbernd, "The 'Normativity of the Future' Approach," 10.

71 Berryman, *Teaching*, 92–101.

juice and cookies, Berryman emphasizes the importance and serenity of the feast in each Godly Play session. Berryman conceived it for the children as "an indirect preparation for their participation in Holy Communion in the church."[72] Clearly, this mystagogical act of communion offers possibilities for introducing children to the eschatological meaning of the eucharistic liturgy.[73] The Godly-Play feast is not only the anticipation of today's children celebrating the eucharist alongside adults in a few years from now. Rather, the feast needs to be framed in a fashion that reflects the anticipation of an alternative world in which God invites all creation to the common table to share a meal together.[74] Children thus get to know a meal that transcends all social hierarchies and discriminatory separations among God's people. It is a meal that is given freely and thus subverts the scarcity and competition that marks the worldly economy which contemporary societies have grown so used to. Celebrating the feast as part of every Godly-Play session in the normative light of God's promised future would be a major step towards encouraging children to become hope-driven actors in their own lives and in society at large.

Conclusion

This chapter set out to explore the role of Christian hope in religious education, particularly through an examination of the Godly Play method, a method of immersive contextual biblical didactics for children. It operationalized biblical eschatology in the *Normativity of the Future* approach as a hermeneutical method for biblical texts, emphasizing the theological understanding of hope as an anticipation of God's promised future. Applying

72 Berryman, *Teaching*, 93.

73 "The worship of the Christian community already celebrates in symbolic form the praise of divine glory, which will find its completion through the eschatological renewal of all creation in the new Jerusalem, which is nothing other than an image of the future kingdom of God." Pannenberg, *Christliche Spiritualität*, 31f. Own translation.

74 "One may hope that the eschatological perspective will establish a new understanding of the meaning of the celebration of the Eucharist as a sign-like anticipation of the future community of a renewed humanity in the Kingdom of God." Pannenberg, *Christliche Spiritualität*, 42. "Thus the Lord's Supper is not to be understood mysteriously and cultically, but eschatologically. The eucharistic community (*Abendmahlsgemeinschaft*) is not the owner of the sacred presence of the absolute, but a waiting, expecting community seeking communion with the coming Lord. Thus Christianity is to be understood as the community of those who, on the basis of Christ's resurrection, are waiting for the kingdom of God and whose lives are determined by this expectation." Moltmann, *Hoffnung*, 301.

it to the core teaching materials of the Godly-Play method, the analysis uncovered a predominant focus on backward-looking narratives rather than future-oriented perspectives. In brief, the Godly Play method suffers from an eschatological deficit.

In the light of these findings, the chapter argues for adjustments to the Godly-Play methodology. It advocates for storytelling that bridges the gap between past narratives and future promises, engaging children as active participants in the unfolding drama of God's plan for humanity. This entails reimagining the content, language, and perspective of Godly-Play lessons to foster a deeper understanding of Christian hope. Furthermore, the paper proposes the Godly-Play feast as a symbolic enactment of eschatological communion, envisioning a world where all are invited to God's table without distinction. By imbuing the feast with eschatological significance, Godly Play can nurture hope-driven agency among children and empower them to embrace their role as co-authors of the future narrative of faith.

Bibliography

Baldermann, Ingo. *Einführung in die biblische Didaktik*. Darmstadt: Wissenschaftliche Buchgesellschaft, 1996.

Berryman, Jerome. *Teaching Godly Play. How to Mentor the Spiritual Development of Children*. Denver, CO: Morehouse Publishing Co., 2009.

Berryman, Jerome. *Godly Play. An Imaginative Approach to Religious Education*. Minneapolis MN: Augsburg Fortress, 1995.

Berryman, Jerome. *The Complete Guide to Godly Play*. Volume 1. *How to Lead Godly Play Lessons*. Denver CO: Morehouse Education Resources, 2002.

Berryman, Jerome. *The Complete Guide to Godly Play*. Volume 2. *14 Presentations for Fall*. Denver CO: Morehouse Education Resources, 2002.

Berryman, Jerome. *The Complete Guide to Godly Play*. Volume 3. *20 Presentations for Winter*. Denver CO: Morehouse Education Resources, 2002.

Berryman, Jerome. *The Complete Guide to Godly Play*. Volume 4. *20 Presentations for Spring*. Denver CO: Morehouse Education Resources, 2002.

Berryman, Jerome. *The Complete Guide to Godly Play*. Volume 8. *15 Presentations*. Denver CO: Morehouse Education Resources, 2012.

Bieringer, Reimund. "Biblical Revelation and Exegetical Interpretation according to Dei Verbum 12." In *Vatican II and Its Legacy*, edited by M. Lamberigts and L. Kenis. BETL 161. Leuven: Peeters, 2002, 25–58.

Bieringer, Reimund. "Dialogical Revelation? On the Reception of Dei Verbum 12 in Verbum Domini." *Asian Horizons* 7:1 (2013): 36–58.

Bieringer, Reimund. "Texts That Create a Future: The Function of Ancient Texts for Theology Today." In *Normativity of the Future. Reading Biblical and Other Authoritative Texts in an Eschatological Perspective*, edited by Reimund Bieringer and Mary Elsbernd. Annua Nuntia Lovaniensia 61. Leuven: Peeters, 2010, 91–116.

Bieringer, Reimund. "The Normativity of the Future: The Authority of the Bible for Theology." In *Normativity of the Future. Reading Biblical and Other Authoritative Texts in an Eschatological Perspective*, edited by Reimund Bieringer and Mary Elsbernd. Annua Nuntia Lovaniensia 61. Leuven: Peeters, 2010, 27–45.

Bieringer, Reimund, and Mary Elsbernd. "Interpreting the Signs of the Time in the Light of the Gospel. Vision and Normativity of the Future." In *Normativity of the Future. Reading Biblical and Other Authoritative Texts in an Eschatological Perspective*, edited by Reimund Bieringer and Mary Elsbernd. Annua Nuntia Lovaniensia 61. Leuven: Peeters, 2010, 47–90.

Bieringer, Reimund. "The 'Normativity of the Future' Approach. Its Roots, Development, Current State and Challenges." In *Normativity of the Future. Reading Biblical and Other Authoritative Texts in an Eschatological Perspective*, edited by Reimund Bieringer and Mary Elsbernd. Annua Nuntia Lovaniensia 61. Leuven: Peeters, 2010, 3–25.

Bloom, Harold. *The Western Canon. The Books and School of the Ages*. New York, NY: Harcourt Brace, 1994.

Bordo, Susan R. *The Flight to Objectivity. Essays on Cartesianism and Culture*. Albany, NY: State University of New York Press, 1987.

Brueggemann, Walter, *Theology of the Old Testament. Testimony, Dispute, Advocacy* (Minneapolis, MN: Fortress Press, 1997).

Crescenzo, Luciano de. *Geschichte der griechischen Philosophie I. Die Vorsokratiker.* Zürich: Diogenes, 1985.

Dillen, Annemie. "Hope, the Motor of Life and of Faith." In *Discovering Practical Theology. Exploring Boundaries*, edited by Annemie Dillen and Stefan Gärtner. Leuven: Peeters, 2020, 221–43.

Elsbernd, Mary, and Reimund Bieringer. *When Love Is Not Enough. A Theo-Ethic of Justice*. Collegeville, MN: Liturgical Press, 2002.

Gadamer, Hans G. *Wahrheit und Methode. Grundzüge Einer Philosophischen Hermeneutik*. Tübingen: Mohr Siebeck, 1960.

Hendrickx, Jeroen, Armin M. Kummer, and Annemie Dillen. "Godly Play Und Die Bibelmüdigkeit Flämischer Jugendlicher." In *"Es ist Schwer Einzuschätzen, wo Man Steht". Jugend und Bibel*, edited by Hanna Roose, Gerhard Büttner, and Thomas Schlag. *Jahrbuch für Kinder- und Jugendtheologie*. Stuttgart: Calwer, 2018.

Hoffman, Lawrence A. "Haggadah of Pessah." In *The Oxford Dictionary of the Jewish Religion*, edited by R. J. Zwi Werblowsky and Geoffrey Wigoder. Oxford and New York, NY: Oxford University Press, 1997, 287–8.

Kummer, Armin M. *Men, Spirituality, and Gender-Specific Biblical Hermeneutics.* Annua Nuntia Lovaniensia 78. Leuven: Peeters, 2019.

Kummer, Armin M. "'You Shall Love YHWH, Your God, with All Your Heart'. Christian Perspectives on Mindfulness Meditation." Uunpublished bachelor degree essay. Faculty of Theology and Religious Studies, KU Leuven, 2014.

McCabe, Herbert. *Law, Love and Language.* London: Sheed & Ward, 1968.

Metz, Johannes Baptist. *A Passion for God. The Mystical-Political Dimension of Christianity.* New York, NY: Paulist, 1998.

Moltmann, Jürgen, Theologie der Hoffnung. Untersuchungen zur Begründung und zu den Konsequenzen einer christlichen Eschatologie (München: Kaiser, 1964).

Moore, Mary Elizabeth Mullino. "Teaching Christian Particularity in a Pluralistic World*." *British Journal of Religious Education* 17:2 (1995): 70–83.

Pannenberg, Wolfhart. *Christliche Spiritualität. Theologische Aspekte.* Kleine Vandenhoeck-Reihe 1519. Göttingen: Vandenhoeck und Ruprecht, 1986.

Robinson, George. *Essential Judaism. A Complete Guide to Beliefs, Customs, and Rituals.* New York, NY: Pocket Books, 2000.

Roebben, Bert. "Generating Hope. The Future of the Teaching Profession in a Globalized World." *Religious Education* 112:3 (2017): 199–206.

Spengler, Oswald. *Der Untergang des Abendlandes. Umrisse einer Morphologie der Weltgeschichte.* München: Beck, 1920.

Walfish, Avraham. "Pesah." In *The Oxford Dictionary of the Jewish Religion*, edited by R. J. Zwi Werblowsky and Geoffrey Wigoder. Oxford and New York, NY: Oxford University Press, 1997, 526–7.

Wengst, Klaus. *Das Regierungsprogramm des Himmelreichs. Eine Auslegung der Bergpredigt in ihrem jüdischen Kontext.* Stuttgart: Kohlhammer, 2010.

Wright, N. T. *The New Testament and the People of God.* Christian Origins and the Question of God 1. London: SPCK, 1992.

Amsterdam University Press

YEARBOOK OF CONTEXTUAL BIBLICAL INTERPRETATION 1 (2024) 77-99
HTTPS://DOI.ORG/10.5117/YCBI2024.006.BADI

"Unbinding" Children's Roles in Philippine Catholic Religious Education

Justin Joseph G. Badion (Ateneo de Manila University, Philippines), jbadion@ateneo.edu, ORCID ID: 0009-0009-4170-7225

Julius Anthony L. Porqueriño (KU Leuven), jules.porquerino@kuleuven.be, ORCID ID: 0000-0002-1019-7746

Abstract

This article employs a childist lens to critically examine the portrayal and roles of children in religious education within Philippine Catholic schools, using the narrative of the Binding of Isaac (Gen. 22:1–19) as a focal point. The study critiques how traditional educational practices in schools perpetuate a systemic silencing of children's voices, leading to epistemic injustice wherein children are relegated to passive roles. By integrating insights from child theology and contextual hermeneutics, the research interprets the Binding of Isaac within the Filipino context, revealing how these practices inhibit children's potential for active participation and critical thinking. The article challenges pedagogical approaches by advocating for educational strategies that balance protective instincts with empowerment. It emphasizes the need for dialogic and inclusive methods that recognize and amplify children's voices as active contributors and co-constructors of their religious learning experiences. Ultimately, this study contributes to the discourse on child theology by offering a contextual critique of religious education practices in Philippine Catholic schools, proposing paradigm shifts that foster a more dynamic and participatory environment that honors children's agency.

Keywords: child theology, childist biblical interpretation, religious education, Philippine Catholic schools

Introduction

This article explores the role of children in Catholic religious education in the Philippines, asking: "What roles do children play in their religious education?" This inquiry challenges the conventional assumption among educators who often make decisions "for the sake of the children."[1] While these decisions are intended to benefit them, Belgian practical theologian Annemie Dillen points out that such practices may not necessarily achieve their intended aim.[2] This perceived disconnect prompts an evaluation of how children are involved in religious education, viewed through the lens of child theology.

This exploration engages with Gen. 22:1–19, the biblical narrative of the Binding of Isaac, through a childist biblical interpretation. It is informed by the critical insights of Australian scholars Sandra Carroll and Antoinette Collins. They note the story's polemic against human sacrifice, highlighting its enduring relevance and the necessity to critically reassess traditional educational roles.[3] By applying the childist lens, we examine how societal and religious constructs often metaphorically "sacrifice" children to adult-imposed principles and values.

For this reflection, we organized our analysis by employing the "three worlds" framework for biblical interpretation. First, we examine the "world behind the text," focusing on the historical and cultural context of Gen. 22:1–19. Next, we explore the "world in front of the text," analyzing its implications for contemporary religious education in Philippine Catholic schools. Finally, we delve into the "world of the text," reflecting on the silencing of Isaac. This analysis seeks to examine and potentially transform the traditional roles assigned to children, advocating for practices that genuinely consider and empower children's voices and experiences in religious education. Echoing Dillen's caution in her reflection on the theology with and for children, we recognize the limitations of our approach. This reflection does not simplify the complex interplay between theological evaluations and societal issues but acknowledges the inherent complexities,

1 Annemie Dillen explains that this notion comes from "the German concept *Kindeswohl*, which refers to the general wellbeing of children and acting 'for the sake of children'". She also notes that works of Marianne Heimbach-Steins and Ana Maria Riedl have contributed to the exploration of this notion. See Dillen, "Children and Christian Theology"; Heimbach-Steins and Riedl, eds., *Kindeswohl*; Riedl, *Ethik*.

2 See Dillen, "For the Sake of the Children?"

3 See Carroll and Collins, "Worlds of the Text," 139.

frictions and messiness involved in educating children.[4] This effort is but one contribution aimed at transforming religious education to truly make it "for the sake of the children."

Childist Biblical Interpretation

In reevaluating traditional narratives of religious education in the Philippines, we adopt a childist biblical interpretation framework grounded in child theology. Influenced by recent developments in children's studies, child theology enables the voices of children to be heard in theological discourse.[5] For this article, German theologian Mirjam Zimmermann's child theology provides a robust foundation. She categorizes engagement into three distinct but interconnected modes: "theology by children," "theology with children," and "theology for children," each shaping how children interact with biblical stories.[6] These modes emphasize children's autonomy in expressing theological insights (theology by children), foster a collaborative relationship between children and adults in religious learning environments (theology with children), and advocate for developing accessible and meaningful theological content for young learners (theology for children). By applying these principles to biblical narratives, we aim to uncover new layers of interpretation that respect and highlight children's perspectives, thus challenging and expanding the traditional roles assigned to them in religious education.

Biblical narratives involving children may hold the key to a potential starting point for reflections that can guide child theology. Of particular note is the Binding of Isaac narrative in Gen. 22:1–19. This narrative is a prime example where a child plays a central role in the story, yet due to an adult-centered focus, the child's perspective and experience are marginalized. Take for instance some of the most common interpretations of this text which problematically hail Abraham as an exemplar of faith for nearly sacrificing Isaac.[7] This notion illustrates how adults, in their service to

4 Dillen, "For the Sake of the Children?," 85.

5 See Dillen, "Children and Christian Theology."

6 Zimmermann, "What Is Children's Theology?"

7 In his own engagement with the text, exegete Jonathan Jacobs explains that: "The Talmudic sages and medieval Jewish biblical commentators alike depict Abraham as journeying to perform the binding with no doubts or misgivings." See Jacobs, "Willing Obedience," 546–47. However, there are also scholars who criticize the position that Abraham's actions constitute abuse of children. See Fretheim, "Binding."

various greater ideals, may discard their ethics—and metaphorically, their children—along with the proverbial bathwater. As explained by philosopher Eddoard Robberechts:

> This text is thus considered to be exemplary of the fact that the believer—the man or woman of religion—must be ready for everything in order to serve God, including to sacrifice his or her most intimate convictions and his or her strongest feelings of humanity and charity. This exegesis, predominant throughout the history of Judaism, but also in the vast majority of cases within Christianity and Islam, has had a seriously damaging impact. Does it not enshrine the peremptory affirmation that religion can demand, in certain critical cases, the sacrifice of ethics? Ethics could thus no longer be said to be the final instance of humanity, but would have to concede primacy to the questionings of the religious sphere, with its demanding quest for the absolute and its radicalism.[8]

Portraying Abraham an exemplar of faith in this narrative not only justifies but even encourages the sacrifice of children.[9] Such kinds of interpretation are a function of a continued trend that puts adults, their actions and concerns, front and center, with little to no regard to the perspective of children in these narratives. By re-examining such narratives through the lens of child theology, we can begin to appreciate and incorporate the child's voice, thereby enriching our theological discourse and practice.

To analyze this narrative, we will employ the methodological triad articulated by Sandra Schneiders in her work *The Revelatory Text*. Schneiders' method includes three interpretative perspectives, represented by three worlds: the "world behind the text" (historical-critical approaches), the "world of the text" (literary-critical approaches), and the "world in front of the text" (reader-response critical approaches).[10]

To integrate a childist perspective into these triads, we pose the following question: What is the potential for critically engaging biblical texts in a specifically childist way? Childist religious education scholar Russell Dalton succinctly explains:

8 Robberechts, "Binding of Isaac," 241.

9 For a challenge to the use of the Biblical text as a book of instruction hinged on exemplarity of various biblical figures, see Lambert, "Biblical Narrative as Ethics."

10 See Schneiders, *Revelatory Text*, 113–22.

> Childist biblical scholarship is not focused on teaching Bible lessons to children or on how children read the Bible. Therefore, one might reasonably ask what relevance such study has for teaching children the Bible. To be clear, for religious educators, the goal of such research is not simply to read what childist biblical scholars have written on a passage and then to lecture on those interpretations to the children in their classes. Rather, the goal is for such research to help conscientize adult religious educators to the childist content and dynamics in biblical texts.[11]

What would a childist version of Schneiders' interpretative triad look like? First, a childist view of the "world behind the text" seeks to reclaim children's voices from a historical-critical perspective. This addresses the methodological challenges arising from historical-critical approaches that often ignore or marginalize the experiences and perspectives of children in antiquity. Second, a childist view of the "world of the text" places children and their concerns at the forefront of literary critical analysis, particularly from a narrative-critical lens. Finally, a childist view of the "world in front of the text" envisions a future where children's experiences are taken seriously, adopting an ideological critical perspective that challenges modern readers, particularly in conscientizing them to the concerns of children.

World Behind the Text: Bindings of Children in Antiquity

In antiquity, children held a secondary role in societal and religious narratives, leading to their marginalization in biblical texts. This secondary status is evident in the limited representation of children's perspectives, which are largely absent or filtered through adult viewpoints. This section explores how historical criticism reveals the marginalization of children in ancient texts and the implications of this on the reading of the Binding of Isaac narrative.

Biblical scholar Reidar Aasgaard, in his examination of children in antiquity and early Christianity, highlights the methodological challenges of studying children in ancient sources.[12] He argues that the voices of children are conspicuously silent, as the sources available are predominantly adult

11 Dalton, "Engaging," 33.

12 See Aasgaard, "Children."

descriptions of children.[13] This underscores the difficulty in accessing authentic child perspectives from ancient times, as they are mediated through the biases and intents of adult authors.

American child theologian Marcia Bunge further discusses the biblical depiction of children as "developing beings who need instruction and guidance."[14] She points to biblical passages that emphasize the responsibility of adults to nurture and educate children, thereby perpetuating a view of children as passive recipients of adult wisdom and care.[15] For instance, passages like Deut. 6:5–7 and Prov. 22:6 highlight the adult duty to impart faith and moral guidance, positioning children as future bearers of religious tradition rather than active participants. This depiction aligns with the view that children, due to their vulnerable status in society at that time, were to be cared for and guided by adults. Children are understood as works-in-progress, "on the way," which neglects their innate capabilities and capacities.

The vulnerability of children in biblical narratives is starkly illustrated through the motif of child sacrifice, where children become victims of adult decisions and actions. Childist scholar Julie Faith Parker provides a grim account of children as sacrificial victims in several biblical stories, showing their vulnerability.[16] Parker notes how children

> fall prey to cannibalism (Lev. 26:29; Deut. 28:53; Jer. 5:17; 19:9) and die violent and untimely deaths (Amos 7:17; Jer. 16:3-4; Ezek. 23:47; 24:21). They are taken captive (Num. 21:29; Deut. 28:32, 41; 1 Sam 30:3; Jer. 48:46; Joel 4:8 [Eng. 3:8]; 2 Chr. 28:8) and sold into slavery (Neh. 5:5; cf. 2 Kgs. 4:1–7).[17]

In these narratives, children are depicted as passive victims of adult decisions and actions. Unable to resist or escape, children were often the victims of such practices, driven by adult decisions rather than their own agency.[18] These accounts highlight the precarious status of children and reflect a broader societal tendency to view children as expendable in pursuit of adult goals.

13 See Aasgaard, "Children," 25.

14 Bunge, "Christian Understandings," 64.

15 See Bunge, "Christian Understandings," 64. See also Gen. 18:19; Deut. 6:5–7; 11:18–19; 31:12–13; Prov. 2:9; 22:6; Ps. 78:4b; Isa. 38:19.

16 See Parker, *Valuable*, 47–8.

17 Parker, *Valuable*, 48.

18 See Garroway, *Growing Up*, 270–71.

The "world behind the text" analysis through a childist lens has shed light on the secondary status of children in ancient literature, emphasizing the dominance of adult agendas. This perspective is vividly illustrated in the Binding of Isaac. Though Isaac's voice is briefly heard when he questions the sacrificial lamb (Gen. 22:7), it is ultimately sidelined by the narrative focus on Abraham's actions. Despite his inquiry, Isaac's perspective and agency are minimized as the story progresses. Reduced to a passive figure, Isaac becomes a mere pawn in the hands of an adult, lacking agency or individual voice. The narrative's portrayal of Isaac as obedient and submissive reflects the broader societal attitudes of antiquity towards children as compliant subjects of adult authority, perpetuating their marginalization and reinforcing their passive roles. The motif of child sacrifice further underscores their vulnerability, where their lives could easily be sacrificed in service of divine appeasement, as seen in Abraham's willingness to sacrifice Isaac.

In conclusion, recognizing the historical situatedness of children's narratives in biblical texts reveals that Isaac was already figuratively "bound" by virtue of being a child, even before his literal binding. By interrogating these narratives through the lens of a critical childist perspective, we gain insight into the complex dynamics of power, agency, and vulnerability that characterize children's experiences, not only in ancient texts, but even and most especially as they continue today.

World in Front of the Text: Contemporary Bindings in Religious Education

Religious education in Philippine Catholic schools is often described as confessional, focused in educating students in the doctrines and traditions of the Catholic faith.[19] This confessional religious education is also designed to be catechetical, insofar as it aims not only to educate in faith (inform), but also to form and transform the students.[20] The goal is for students to deepen their faith commitment or adopt Catholic values through this education. According to Filipino education scholar Johnny Go, it is commonly believed that Catholic schools in the Philippines are mandated to "preach and teach."[21]

19 See Go, *Religious Education*, 9–20; Castillo and Sarmiento, "Systematic Review," 7; Baring, "Experiencing Religion," 14.

20 See Groome, *Will There Be Faith?*, 89–120.

21 Go, *Religious Education*, 19.

This approach can create modern-day "bindings" similar to those in the Binding of Isaac. For example, just as Isaac is bound by his father in Gen. 22:9, representing the imposition of adult authority over a child's agency, rigid teaching methods can bind students to a singular interpretation of faith. Isaac's question in Gen. 22:7 demonstrates a moment of curiosity and agency, which is ultimately overshadowed by Abraham's authoritative response. Similarly, in religious education, children's questions and critical engagement with the material are often stifled by overemphasis on doctrinal instruction and grading of assessments. To move towards "unbinding," educators should create spaces where children's voices are not only heard but are integral to the learning process. This shift aligns with the broader biblical theme of liberation and empowerment, as illustrated by God's intervention in Gen. 22:11–13 to prevent the sacrifice of Isaac, symbolically unbinding him and allowing the possibility of reclaiming his agency and voice.

While this confessional approach has strengths, particularly in Catholic schools where the majority of students are Catholic, it relies heavily on what Filipino theologian Rebecca Cacho calls "classical methods."[22] These methods are systematic and logical, ideal for presenting doctrine clearly, but they can be restrictive when a single faith perspective dominates, as they may not encourage exploration beyond established viewpoints. This approach often positions the teacher as the sole authority, dictating discourse while students remain passive recipients in lecture-driven classes that emphasize information absorption rather than active engagement.

Reliance on these classical methods places children into predefined roles within religious education. Upon closer examination, these roles function as bindings, imposing limitations that hinder children's ability to fully express and develop their identity, agency and competencies within the religious education classroom. Each role—child as the universal child, child as a blank slate, and child as a vulnerable passive object—illustrates a different aspect of restrictive educational practices in the Philippines that hinder rather than foster children's spiritual development.

Child as the Universal Child: Binding the Child's Identity

The one-size-fits-all teaching strategy in religious education is indicative of an underlying perception of children as the "universal child." Australian scholar Jan Grajczonek notes that the "universal child" concept assumes

22 Cacho, "Making," 166.

uniform developmental stages for all children, ignoring their cultural, social, political and individual differences.[23] This idea is reflected in the Binding of Isaac, where Isaac is depicted as a compliant, silent figure whose identity and agency are shaped entirely by his father's actions and the expectations of the adult world. Isaac's role in the story aligns with the idea of the universal child—viewed not as an individual with unique perspectives and capabilities, but as a representative of a generalized, passive childhood. For Grajczonek, these assumptions stem from developmental theories like those of Piaget, Kohlberg, and Erikson.[24] These theories have traditionally shaped Philippine education with age- or developmentally-appropriate educational policies and curricula.[25] Activities designed for children are based on generalized stages of development rather than individual capabilities or cultural contexts. Relying on universal models can bind children's religious identities, restricting their engagement with religious texts and stifling spiritual development, much like how Isaac's identity and agency are bound by the expectations placed upon him in the narrative.

Another factor that reduces children to the "universal child" in education is the over-emphasis on standardized measurements and outcomes. Australian education scholar Brendan Hyde characterizes this phenomenon as the neoliberal discourse of performativity.[26] Neoliberal policies emphasize quantifiable success, often sidelining the spiritual, emotional, and cultural aspects crucial in religious contexts. In the Philippines, curricula that include religious education adhere to this performative model, as seen in the influence of the outcomes-based and learner-centered framework of *Understanding by Design*.[27] For example, the curriculum map for religious education in Catholic schools includes performance and faith standards, target learning competencies, target values, and specified year-level topics.[28] While structured and measurable, this approach risks oversimplifying children's spiritual experiences by prioritizing measurable indicators such as memorization of doctrines. Hyde's critique highlights how performativity not only constrains the educational experience but also stifles children's ability to develop and express their unique spiritual

23 See Grajczonek, "How Shall We Know Them?"

24 For an illustration of the stage theories, see McLeod, "Jean Piaget's Theory"; McLeod, "Kohlberg's Stages"; McLeod, "Erik Erikson's Stages."

25 See Department of Education, "MATATAG Curriculum," 37.

26 See Hyde, "Silenced."

27 See Wiggins and McTighe, *Understanding*.

28 See CEAP National Christian Formation Commission, *Integrated*.

identities, effectively silencing the diverse voices and experiences that do not conform to standardized expectations.[29]

Child as Blank Slate: Binding the Child's Capability

The "universal child" leads to perceptions of children as "not-yet" or "lacking". This perception binds their competences. In Gen. 22:1-19, Isaac's role is similarly constrained. As Isaac is bound by Abraham, not only is his physical movement restricted, but his potential for action or expression is figuratively negated. This act of binding reflects the broader tendency to view children as incomplete beings, whose capabilities must be directed by adults. This perspective mirrors the "banking model" of education, critiqued by Brazilian educator Paulo Freire, where children are seen as passive recipients of adult knowledge.[30] Teachers act as depositors of information, while children passively receive and memorize content. By conceptualizing education as a simple deposit-and-withdrawal process, it disregards children's capabilities to explore and be active co-creators of their learning. The narrative of Isaac being bound thus serves as a metaphor for the limitations imposed on children's agency and capability in school settings.

The adoption of the "banking model" in religious education is emblematic of the traditional, unidirectional model of religious socialization critiqued by Dillen.[31] This model reflects and presupposes a "deficit approach" to children, viewing them primarily as recipients of adult knowledge.[32] This perspective restricts their competencies, relegating their role to that of passive recipients of predetermined content. It adheres to an adult-centric perspective that views children mainly as future adults, thus overlooking their current competencies and needs. This perspective not only diminishes their individuality and competences by focusing on what children do not have yet but also undermines their potential as active participants in their own religious learning. In doing so, it disregards the inherent capabilities of children to explore, question, and co-create their learning, thus maintaining a restrictive hold on their intellectual and spiritual development.

29 Hyde, "Silenced," 20.

30 See Freire, *Pedagogy*, 72.

31 See Dillen, "Religious Participation," 40–3; Dillen, "Aren't They Too Young?," 157–62.

32 See Dillen, "Between Heroism."

In the Philippines, a pervasive deficit view underestimates children's capacity for higher-order thinking. Filipino philosopher Peter Elicor points out the need to examine adult responses to children, often dismissive, like "*wala ka pa masyadong alam sa buhay*" ("you do not have much experience in life yet") or "*hindi ka pa namulat sa katotohanan*" ("you have not been exposed to the truth yet").[33] Such attitudes reinforce the belief that children must mature before engaging in meaningful inquiry. These attitudes stifle children's capacity for critical thinking and exploration.

These cultural attitudes manifest in religious education, binding children's competences in multiple ways. Dismissing children's questions not only suppresses their intellectual curiosity but also signals that their current thinking is inadequate. For example, in Gen. 22:7–8, Isaac's question reflects his capacity for observation and critical thinking, yet is subtly brushed aside by Abraham. Similarly in religious education, there is a tendency to overlook or undervalue children's intellectual contributions. Abraham's dismissal within the narrative exemplifies how children's voices can be marginalized, reinforcing a dynamic where their curiosity and developing understanding are suppressed rather than nurtured. This parallels the overemphasis on memorization in religious education, where children's opportunities for personal interpretations and critical engagement with the materials are similarly negated.[34]

Moreover, American practical theologians Karen-Marie Yust and Erin Reibel note that many religious education materials limit learning by promoting a single "main point" with predetermined responses, treating children as empty vessels to be filled with religious content.[35] This approach sacrifices critical thinking for rote learning of Catholic teachings, neglecting education's dynamic and interactive nature.[36] Contrasting sharply with more inclusive methods, traditional theological views treat children as "not-yet-adults," needing faith socialization, and ignore their existing capabilities. By perpetuating the notion that children are incomplete receptacles of religious content, these outdated perspectives restrict their competences in religious education.

33 Elicor, "Filipino Children," 70.

34 See Cornelio, "Rethinking."

35 Yust and Reibel, "Innovations," 504.

36 See Go, *Religious Education*, 18–19.

Child as Vulnerable Passive Object: Binding the Child's Agency

In Gen. 22:9, Abraham binds Isaac and lays him on the altar, a moment that can be interpreted as the stripping away of Isaac's agency. Although Isaac has previously showed signs of awareness and inquiry, such as in Gen. 22:7 when he asks about the lamb for the sacrifice, his voice and actions are absent when he is bound. This act reduces Isaac to a passive recipient of his father's will, exemplifying how children's agency can be overshadowed by adult authority. The subsequent verse, Gen. 22:10, where Abraham takes the knife to sacrifice his son, highlights Isaac's extreme vulnerability. At this point, Isaac's life hangs in the balance, completely subject to his father's faith-driven actions. This moment exemplifies the power imbalance between them. Abraham's readiness to wield the knife over his bound son illustrates not just his obedience to God, but also how he perceives Isaac—a child whose agency is subsumed under his will.

Despite this dynamic, there is space to consider what Isaac might have learned about obedience and faith from his father. While Isaac's agency appears suppressed, he witnesses Abraham's profound act of faith and obedience to God. This experience could serve as a powerful, albeit complex, lesson for Isaac about the nature of faith—one that involves trust and submission, but also an understanding of the responsibilities that come with spiritual commitment. This perspective introduces a critical nuance to the interpretation of Isaac's role, suggesting that what may seem like passive vulnerability could also be an opportunity for learning and spiritual growth, particularly when the act of obedience is framed within a context that encourages reflection and dialogue. Thus, the narrative of Isaac can be seen as not only a story of power dynamics but also a formative moment in which a child learns about the complexities of faith and obedience, ideally under the guidance of a supportive and understanding figure.

Parallel to Isaac's experience, children in Philippine religious education are often positioned as vulnerable passive objects under teacher authority. This view, strongly influenced by the protective paradigm outlined by Dillen, advocates for a form of religious education that serves as a safeguard against the perceived secular threats to children's spiritual development.[37] Grajczonek's research on church documents supports this portrayal of children as inherently unable to cope with ambiguous or harmful secular

37 Dillen, "Aren't They Too Young?," 158–60.

influences.[38] Consequently, children are considered in need of protection, with a focus on maintaining spiritual integrity over nurturing their theological autonomy. This approach insists on a singular religious tradition, suggesting that without it, children might adopt worldviews dominated by secularization, materialism and consumerism.[39] As a result, the educational strategy insulates rather than engages, controlling children's interaction with religious content to ensure adherence to the faith.

This protective stance in education is further reinforced by broader cultural attitudes in the Philippines, which view childhood as a period of vulnerability requiring careful oversight. Filipino psychologist Liane Alampay highlights how these cultural perspectives influence educational practices.[40] Filipino parents often view young children as lacking sense and self-control, necessitating a protective approach that extends into educational settings.[41] This cultural perspective results in educational practices where religious education teachers, much like Filipino mothers, exhibit overprotectiveness, viewing it as an integral expression of educational and spiritual care. Consequently, religious education tends to discourage inquisitiveness and direct children towards passive learning, emphasizing the acquisition of a safe, prescribed set of beliefs and values. This nurturing yet restrictive environment limits children's opportunities to engage critically with theological concepts, inadvertently constraining their agency and stifling their potential for a deep personal connection with their faith.

The binding of children's agency in religious education is also evident in pre-digested narratives that simplify complex religious teachings, akin to a parent pre-chewing food for easier digestion. While intended for protection, this method risks oversimplification and limits children's capacity to engage with and interpret religious content on their own terms. This is similar to what Dillen calls as "power over," which is prevalent in religious education. In the context of education, "power over" takes place when educators dictate learning content and methods, reducing students to mere recipients of information.[42] This is partly driven by the fear of possibly exposing children to dangerous influences. Even in more interactive settings,

38 See Grajczonek, "How Shall We Know Them?," 9–18; Grajczonek, "Construction," 40–47.

39 See Gutiérrez, "Catholic Schools," 722.

40 See Alampay, "Parenting," 105–21.

41 Alampay, "Parenting," 111.

42 Dillen, "Empowering Children," 5–6.

adult interpretations dominate, curtailing children's input and reinforcing a passive reception of faith.

It is crucial to recognize that "power over" need not be entirely negative if balanced appropriately with "power with" and "power within." While "power over" provides necessary guidance and protection, especially for vulnerable children, it should be complemented with opportunities for children to exercise their agency and engage in collaborative learning environments. As Filipino practical theologian Julius Porqueriño notes, "power over" can be beneficial in guiding children through complex spiritual and ethical issues, where adult intervention is necessary to correct misguided beliefs or protect them from harmful influences.[43] In this way, "power over" can also serve as a tool for teaching valuable lessons in obedience and faith, much like Isaac's experience under Abraham's guidance. While Isaac's agency appears limited, his obedience to Abraham and the faith he witnesses in his father could be formative experiences, teaching him about trust, commitment, and spiritual responsibility. Nevertheless, this authority should not overshadow the need for a balanced approach. By allowing children to participate in the learning process ("power with") and nurturing their inner strengths ("power within"), religious education can move beyond mere protection and foster a more dynamic, participatory, and empowering experience for children. This balanced approach ensures that while children are protected from potential harm, they are also empowered to explore and interpret their faith independently, leading to deeper personal connections with their spirituality.

World of the Text: Unheard Voices in Genesis 22:1-19

This section employs a narrative critical and intertextual lens to explore children's experiences in the Binding of Isaac story, particularly in relation to adult actions. This can be accomplished from a childist approach that aims to foreground children's perspectives. This approach allows readers to discern the emotional and psychological implications of the events depicted.[44]

American philosopher Aviezer Tucker offers a poignant exploration of Isaac's ordeal:

43 See Porqueriño, "Nurturing Children's Spirituality," 90–93.

44 See Dalton, "Engaging," 32.

> From Isaac's point of view, his father, Abraham, decided to murder him premeditatively, lied to him once, and concealed the truth another time, while making him carry the woods for his own immolation. Then, at the last moment, after his father ties him up and prepares to slaughter him, Abraham sacrifices a ram instead.[45]

Despite the trauma inflicted upon him, the Bible remains silent regarding Isaac's response, leaving his emotional state open to our speculation as readers.[46]

The text's silence on Isaac's emotions emphasizes its focus on Abraham's faith and obedience, overshadowing the child's life-threatening experience at the hands of his father. This absence of Isaac's voice highlights a broader pattern within biblical narratives where children's perspectives are marginalized in favour of adult concerns and agenda.

An intertextual analysis reveals how Isaac's fate in Gen. 22:1–14 is intertwined with that of his half-brother Ishmael in Gen. 21:14–20, highlighting the sacrificial undertones and repeated patterns in Abraham's actions. Aviezer Tucker's analysis reveals the parallel injustices inflicted upon Ishmael and his mother, Hagar, as they are callously expelled into the desert at Sarah's behest.[47] In both narratives, the children rely on divine intervention—God provides a well for Ishmael and Hagar in the wilderness (Gen. 21:19) and a ram for Isaac's sacrifice (Gen. 22:13). These scenes highlight the repeated patterns of vulnerability and potential sacrifice in the lives of Abraham's sons, showing deep interconnection between their fates as shaped by their father's decisions. Both stories feature how an adult's devotion to their god lead to child sacrifices.

Biblical scholar Ed Noort, in his examination of the two related narratives, underscores the interrelatedness between the expulsion of Ishmael and the near-sacrifice of Isaac. Both narratives share formal and thematic parallels, portraying the vulnerability of promise-bearing sons facing imminent death.[48] The comparison of these two stories highlights a recurring theme in biblical texts where children's lives are jeopardized due to adult decisions—often faith-driven—without a deep exploration of the children's own experiences and perspectives.

45 Tucker, "Sins," 35.

46 See Tucker, "Sins," 35.

47 Tucker, "Sins," 36.

48 Noort, "Genesis 22," 5.

The striking silence about Isaac's emotions in the Binding of Isaac narrative sharply highlights the biblical text's focus on Abraham's faith, overshadowing the child's experience. This absence invites adults to reflect critically on their own practices: How might our own priorities and decisions, under the guise of higher purposes, inadvertently silence the voices of children in our care? Such a question not only prompts a re-evaluation of how we interpret sacred texts but also challenges us to ensure that children's perspectives are heard and valued in educational settings.

Towards Unbinding: A Critical Response and Practical Implications

In our childist reading of Gen. 22, Isaac's silence emerges as a poignant motif, inviting deeper exploration. This silence begs a critical question: was Isaac silent or was he silenced? This analysis reveals a narrative pattern reflecting broader societal dynamics where children's voices are systematically sidelined or stifled. Silencing Isaac symbolizes not only the historical marginalization of child characters, but also highlights a systematic epistemic injustice prevalent in contemporary educational settings.[49]

In considering the role of children in this narrative, it might be tempting to conclude that Isaac, as a child, was simply silenced by adult authority in the service of God. However, biblical scholar Terence Fretheim urges caution against such a reductive interpretation. Fretheim notes that Isaac was given a voice in the narrative—he asks a crucial question and receives a caring response from his father.[50] This interaction suggests that Isaac's later silence in the story could indicate obedience and trust, reflecting the trust Abraham himself placed in God. Yet, Fretheim also acknowledges the discomfort this interpretation brings, as Isaac endured a potentially traumatizing experience.[51] While Isaac's silence might be understood as a voluntary expression of faith, modelled on his father's unwavering trust in God, it could equally be seen as an enforced silence, possibly due to fear and power dynamics. Fretheim raises the intriguing possibility that the events on Mount Moriah may have strained the relationship between Abraham

49 The term "epistemic injustice" was coined by British philosopher Miranda Fricker to describe the various forms of systemic oppression and distortions that affect marginalized groups in their roles and capacities related to knowledge bearing and knowledge production. See Fricker, *Epistemic Injustice*.

50 See Fretheim, "Binding," 92.

51 See Fretheim, "Binding," 92.

and Isaac, suggesting that the experience would likely have left a lasting impact on Isaac's perception of his father.[52]

Within this silence and perceived passivity, there is room to explore the lessons Isaac might have internalized about obedience and faith. While it is crucial to challenge the dynamics that silence children, it is equally important to acknowledge that obedience, when framed within a supportive and dialogic context, can be a valuable aspect of spiritual formation. By understanding obedience as a collaborative process—where children are guided rather than dominated—we can unbind them from restrictive roles and empower them to see obedience not as blind submission but as a meaningful engagement with their faith. This perspective aligns with the balanced approach proposed earlier, where "power over" is tempered by "power with," ensuring that children's spiritual journeys are both guided and self-directed.

This oppressive silencing aligns with feminist philosopher Kristie Dotson's concept of "testimonial quieting." This occurs when the audience, often adults, fails to recognize a speaker, like a child, as a legitimate knower, undermining their contributions.[53] Drawing from the work of Patricia Hill Collins, Dotson shows how "controlling images"—persistent stereotypes—facilitate testimonial quieting by promoting unfair treatment and negative assessments.[54] For example, within the Philippine educational system, "controlling images" such as viewing the child as a blank slate or passive object may lead to testimonial quieting in classrooms. Drawing from the work of British philosopher Miranda Fricker, we can identify this as a kind of testimonial epistemic injustice where

> hearers fail to exercise any critical awareness regarding the prejudice that is distorting their perception of the speaker, so that the distorted spontaneous deliverance of their testimonial sensibility is left unchecked.[55]

Fricker discusses not only testimonial injustice, but also hermeneutical epistemic injustice, which she defines as the "injustice of having some significant area of one's social experience obscured from collective understanding owing to persistent and wide-ranging hermeneutical

52 See Fretheim, "Binding," 92.
53 Dotson, "Tracking," 242–43
54 See Dotson, "Tracking," 242–43; see also Collins, *Black*, 69–96.
55 Fricker, *Epistemic Injustice*, 89.

marginalization."[56] This occurs when a marginalized group's experiences are "inadequately conceptualized and so ill-understood"—by themselves or by others — because these experiences do not align with existing conceptual frameworks, leading to their misunderstanding or neglect.[57] Children are often victims of hermeneutical epistemic injustice, as adults, distanced from their own childhoods, struggle to relate to and understand children's concerns and perspectives.

Fricker's perspective resonates with the Filipino context, particularly in challenging prevailing parenting practices that dismiss children's inquiries as taboo or inappropriate. Filipino parenting often involves shielding children from perceived adult, mature, and taboo themes, believed to potentially taint their innocence. This leads to typical dismissive responses such as "*baka malason lang ang isip mo*" ("your mind could be poisoned") and "*wala ka pa sa tamang gulang para malaman 'yan*" ("you are not yet in the right age to know that"). While these responses may seem suitable in certain contexts, they dismiss children's questions, silencing them rather than sustaining their curiosity.[58] It is imperative, therefore, to challenge and dismantle these entrenched norms to foster an environment where children's voices are acknowledged and valued.

In religious education, American practical theologian Joyce Ann Mercer has observed both forms of epistemic injustice. Children face testimonial epistemic injustice when their spiritual insights are dismissed due to their age, undermining their credibility as knowers.[59] For instance, when teachers enforce a single "correct" interpretation of biblical stories, they often overlook and silence children's personal interpretations. Hermeneutical epistemic injustice occurs when significant gaps in the collective interpretive resources leave groups, such as children, unable to fully understand their experiences.[60] In religious education, this manifests as children lacking the language or concepts to link their socio-economic realities with their faith or engage with complex religious texts. This lack of resources hinders children from understanding and expressing their spiritual and ethical dilemmas, a direct result of educational strategies that favour protection over empowering them to explore and develop their faith autonomously.

56 Fricker, *Epistemic Injustice*, 154.
57 Fricker, *Epistemic Injustice*, 6–7.
58 See Elicor, "Filipino Children," 70.
59 Mercer, "Epistemic Injustice," 1.
60 Mercer, "Epistemic Injustice," 2.

Interpreting the Binding of Isaac through a childist lens shows how the narrative symbolizes the systematic sacrificial ethos imposed on children in modern educational systems, extending beyond its historical and religious contexts. By foregrounding Isaac's silenced voice, this critical perspective challenges readers to confront the pervasive silencing of children in educational settings. Using reader-response criticism, this analysis sparks a critical dialogue intended to liberate children's voices in religious education, challenging and changing traditional dynamics. It seeks to dismantle entrenched power dynamics and address epistemic injustices, thereby paving the way for an educational paradigm shift. This envisioned shift aims to transform children from passive recipients into active participants in religious education, co-constructing meaning and fostering a more inclusive and empowering pedagogical praxis that genuinely embraces their experiences.

Conclusion: Navigating the Tensions

Drawing from the childist reading of Gen. 22, we ask: What vision does the Binding of Isaac project for the future of children? The previous sections have illustrated how current educational practices in Philippine Catholic religious education often bind children in restrictive roles, such as the universal child, the blank slate, and the vulnerable passive object. While these roles may be well-intentioned, they limit children's identity, competence, agency, and overall growth within religious education. However, simply reversing these roles may not be the solution, as it could still trap children within another rigid framework. Instead of merely individualizing education—which might inadvertently bind children further—we propose a balanced educational approach.

To address the "universal child," educators could balance their focus not only on who the child can become but also on who the child is in the present moment. Beyond relying solely on developmental theories for guidance, educators could also consider Bronfrenbrenner's ecological systems theory, which recognizes the multiple layers of context influencing a child's development.[61] This perspective helps move beyond seeing children as "blank slates" to be filled with knowledge or as "vulnerable passive objects" needing protection. For the "blank slate," balancing knowledge transmission with exploration empowers children to co-construct their learning, encouraging

61 For a detailed understanding of the socio-ecological theory of Bronfenbrenner, see Bronfenbrenner, "Experimental Ecology." Also see Vélez-Agosto et al., "Bioecological Theory Revision."

them to engage with religious narratives on their own terms. This approach fosters a richer learning environment by incorporating children's unique interpretations and experiences. For the "vulnerable passive object," balancing protection with empowerment shifts the focus from merely shielding children to enabling them to navigate and interpret complex religious experiences and ethical issues independently. This shift encourages children to develop a personal connection with their faith, transforming them from passive recipients to engaged participants.

As we continue to explore the evolving landscape of Catholic religious education, it becomes increasingly clear that reimagining a future where children are not confined by restrictive roles is an ongoing challenge. Drawing on Grajczonek's insight that children, created in the image and likeness of God, deserve the same respect and treatment as adults, this reflection invites us to reconsider our educational practices.[62] However, this is but one step in a broader conversation—one that calls us not just to advocate for children, but to truly listen to them, acknowledging their agency and dignity as active participants in their education and spiritual development. Embracing a childist approach means moving beyond speaking for children and continuously seeking ways to value and amplify their voices in meaningful ways.

Bibliography

Aasgaard, Reidar. "Children in Antiquity and Early Christianity. Research History and Central Issues." *Familia* 33 (2006): 23–46.

Alampay, Liane Peña. "Parenting in the Philippines." In *Parenting Across Cultures. Childrearing, Motherhood and Fatherhood in Non-Western Cultures.*, edited by Helaine Selin. Vol. 7. *Science Across Cultures: The History of Non-Western Science.* Dordrecht: Springer, 2014, 105–21.

Baring, Rito V. "Experiencing Religion. Post-Colonial Views for Religious Education." *Religions* 13:1 (2022): 14.

Baring, Rito V. "The State of Religious Education in the Philippines. A Review of Literature." *Hapág* 12:2 (2015): 139–59.

Bronfenbrenner, Urie, 'Toward an Experimental Ecology of Human Development', *American Psychologist* 32 (1977) 513–31.

Bunge, Marcia J. "Christian Understandings of Children. Central Biblical Themes and Resources." In *Children, Adults, and Shared Responsibilities. Jewish, Christian*

62 See Grajczonek, "Construction," 42–44.

and Muslim Perspectives, edited by Marcia J. Bunge. Cambridge: Cambridge University Press, 2012, 59–78.

Cacho, Rebecca G. "Making Religious Instruction and Values Formation Relevant to 21st Century Learners." *Hapág* 12:2 (2015): 161–72.

Carroll, Sandra, and Antoinette Collins. "The Worlds of the Text. A Contextual Approach to Scripture for Religious Educators." *Journal of Religious Education* 62 (2015): 129–39.

Castillo, Fides del, and Philip Joseph Sarmiento. "A Systematic Review on Spiritual Modeling. Opportunities and Challenges in Religious Education." *International Journal of Christianity & Education* 26:1 (March 2022): 6–17.

Catholic Bishops' Conference of the Philippines. *Catechism for Filipino Catholics*. Manila: Episcopal Commission on Catechesis and Catholic Education, Word & Life Publications, 1997.

Catholic Bishops' Conference of the Philippines. *New National Catechetical Directory for the Philippines*. Manila: Episcopal Commission for Catechesis and Catholic Education, 2007.

CEAP National Christian Formation Commission. *Integrated Curriculum of Christian Living Education, Good Manners & Right Conduct and Values Education for K to 12 Basic Education*. Quezon City: Rex Bookstore, 2020.

Collins, Patricia Hill. *Black Feminist Thought. Knowledge, Consciousness, and the Politics of Empowerment.* 2nd edition. New York, NY: Routledge, 2000.

Cornelio, Jayeel. "Rethinking Religious Education." *Rappler*. Accessed October 10, 2017. https://www.rappler.com/voices/thought-leaders/184761-rethinking-religious-education/.

Dalton, Russell W. "Engaging Childist Biblical Interpretation and Reading Studies to Enhance Children's Bible Lessons." *Religious Education* 119:1 (2024): 31–42.

Department of Education. "MATATAG Curriculum. General Shaping Paper." Department of Education, 2023. Accessed April 20, 2024. https://www.deped.gov.ph/matatagcurriculumk147/.

Dillen, Annemie. "Aren't They Too Young? The Challenge of Hermeneutical and Interreligious Learning in Catholic Religious Education. A Flemish Perspective." In *Global Perspectives on Catholic Religious Education in Schools*, edited by T. Buchanan and Adrian-Mario Gellel. Cham: Springer, 2015, 155–65.

Dillen, Annemie. "Between Heroism and Deficit: Challenges to Research on Children's Spirituality from a Christian Theological Standpoint." *Concilium* 5 (2007): 57–68.

Dillen, Annemie. "Children and Christian Theology." In *St. Andrews Encyclopaedia of Theology*, edited by Brendan Wolfe, Steve Holmes, Andrew Mein, Judith Wolfe, N. T. Wright, Rebekah Dyer, Oliver B. Langworthy, and Mikael Leidenhag.

29 February 2024. Accessed April 16, 2024. https://www.saet.ac.uk/Christianity/ChildrenandChristianTheology.

Dillen, Annemie. "Empowering Children in Religious Education. Rethinking Power Dynamics." *Journal of Religious Education* 59:3 (2011): 4–11.

Dillen, Annemie. "For the Sake of the Children? Theology, Care and Children." *Hapág* 16:1-2 (2019): 85–97.

Dillen, Annemie. "Religious Participation of Children as Active Subjects. Toward a Hermeneutical-communicative Model of Religious Education in Families with Young Children." *International Journal of Children's Spirituality* 12:1 (April 2007): 37–49.

Dotson, Kristie. "Tracking Epistemic Violence, Tracking Practices of Silencing." *Hypatia* 26:2 (Spring 2011): 236–57.

Elicor, Peter Paul E. "Are Filipino Children Too Young to Do Philosophy?." *Kritike* 18:1 (March 2024): 66–87.

Freire, Paulo *Pedagogy of the Oppressed.* Translated by Myra Bergman Ramos. Reprinted Thirtieth Anniversary edition. New York, NY: Bloomsbury, 2014.

Fretheim, Terence E. "The Binding of Isaac and the Abuse of Children (Genesis 22)." *Lutheran Theological Journal* 42:1 (August 2007): 84–92.

Fricker, Miranda. *Epistemic Injustice. Power and the Ethics of Knowing.* New York, NY: Oxford University Press, 2007.

Garroway, Kristine Henriksen. *Growing Up in Ancient Israel. Children in Material Culture and Biblical Texts.* Atlanta, GA: SBL Press, 2018.

Go, Johnny C. *Religious Education from a Critical Realist Perspective. Sensus Fidei and Critical Thinking.* Abingdon: Routledge, 2019.

Grajczonek, Jan. "How Shall We Know Them? Part 1 – the Construction of 'Child' and 'Childhood' in Official Church Educational Documents." *Journal of Religious Education* 58:2 (2010): 9–18.

Grajczonek, Jan. "The Construction of 'Child' and 'Childhood' in Official Church Educational Documents Part 2: Implications for Early Childhood Religious Educators." *Journal of Religious Education* 59:4 (2011): 40–47.

Groome, Thomas. *Will There Be Faith? A New Vision for Educating and Growing Disciples.* New York, NY: HarperOne, 2011.

Gutiérrez, Angelina L.V. "Catholic Schools in the Philippines. Beacons of Hope in Asia." In *International Handbook of Catholic Education. Challenges for School Systems in the 21st Century*, edited by Gerald Grace and Joseph O'Keefe. Dordrecht: Springer Netherlands, 2007, 709–23.

Heimbach-Steins, Marianne, and Anna Maria Riedl, eds. *Kindeswohl Zwischen Anspruch Und Wirklichkeit. Theorie Und Praxis Im Gespräch.* Paderborn: Schöningh, 2017.

Hyde, Brendan. "Silenced by Performativity. The Child's Right to a Spiritual Voice in an Age of Neoliberal Educational Imperatives." *International Journal of Children's Spirituality* 26:1-2 (2021): 9–23.

Jacobs, Jonathan. "Willing Obedience with Doubts. Abraham at the Binding of Isaac." *Vetus Testamentum* 60:4 (2010): 546–59.

Lambert, David. "Biblical Narrative as Ethics? The Limits of Exemplarity in Ancient Jewish Literature." *Dead Sea Discoveries* 28:2S (2021): 423–47.

Mercer, Joyce Ann. "Epistemic Injustice and Religious Education." *Religious Education* 117:1 (2022): 1–3.

Noort, Ed. "Genesis 22. Human Sacrifice and Theology in the Hebrew Bible." In *The Sacrifice of Isaac. The Aqedah (Genesis 22) and Its Interpretations*, edited by Ed Noort and Eibert Tigchelaar. Leiden: Brill, 2002, 1–20.

Parker, Julie Faith. *Valuable and Vulnerable. Children in the Hebrew Bible, Especially the Elisha Cycle.* Providence, RI: Brown Judaic Studies, 2013.

Porqueriño, Julius. "Nurturing Children's Spirituality. Insights for Catholic Schools in the Philippines." *MST Review* 26:1 (2024): 60–98.

Riedl, Anna Maria. *Ethik an Den Grenzen Der Souveränität. Christliche Sozialethik Im Dialog Mit Judith Butler Unter Berücksichtigung Des Kindeswohlbegriffs.* Paderborn: Schöningh, 2017.

Robberechts, Edouard "The Binding of Isaac. A Different Jewish Reading." In *The Quest for a Common Humanity. Human Dignity and Otherness in the Religious Traditions of the Mediterranean*, edited by Katell Berthelot and Matthias Morgenstern. Leiden: Brill, 2011, 239–54.

Schneiders, Sandra M. *The Revelatory Text. Interpreting the New Testament as Sacred Scripture.* 2nd edition, Collegeville, MN: Liturgical Press, 1999.

Tucker, Aviezer "Sins of Our Fathers. A Short History of Religious Child Sacrifice." *Zeitschrift für Religions- und Geistesgeschichte* 51:1 (1999): 30–47.

Vélez-Agosto, Nicole M., José G. Soto-Crespo, Mónica Vizcarrondo-Oppenheimer, Stephanie Vega-Molina, and Cynthia García Coll. "Bronfenbrenner's Bioecological Theory Revision. Moving Culture From the Macro Into the Micro." *Perspectives on Psychological Science* 12:5 (2017): 900–10.

Wiggins, Grant P., and Jay McTighe. *Understanding by Design.* Expanded 2nd edition. Alexandria, VA: Association for Supervision and Curriculum Development, 2008.

Yust, Karen-Marie, and Erin Reibel. "Innovations in Children's Spiritual Nurture." *Religious Education* 118:5 (2023): 504–16.

Zimmermann, Mirjam. "What Is Children's Theology? Children's Theology as Theological Competence. Development, Differentiation, Methods." *HTS Teologiese Studies/Theological Studies* 71:3 (March 11, 2015): a2848.

Amsterdam University Press

YEARBOOK OF CONTEXTUAL BIBLICAL INTERPRETATION 1 (2024) 100-115
HTTPS://DOI.ORG/10.5117/YCBI2024.007.RENK

Religion, Worldview and Diversity in School: What to Expect from Teachers?

Dr. Erik Renkema, educational theologian and identity consultant for Verus, the Association for Catholic and Christian Education in the Netherlands

Abstract

Child theology aims at focusing on religious questions and experiences of children. Literature underlines this as a dominant dimension of religious dialogue and the development of a personal identity of children. In primary and secondary schools, the connection between personal identity and dialogue in the classroom, in the context of worldview diversity, means that teachers need to emphasize the religious questions and views of children themselves.

What does the focus on personal identity of children and worldview dialogue mean for the role of teachers to foster the dialogue about the theological perspectives of children? This article builds on an hermeneutical communicative perspective on this role that is significant for teachers who work in the context of religious diversity. The presupposition is that child theology requires specific and professional characteristics of teachers. The author distinguishes five characteristics: Translator, Imaginator, Moderator, Explorer, Source. This perspective invites the reader to reflect on the question what and how professionals in child theology contribute to the development of children's identity.

Keywords: Child theology, hermeneutical communicative perspective, worldview education, citizenship education, diversity, teacher roles.

The Religious Context of Education in the Netherlands

Dutch schools find themselves, religiously speaking, in a context characterized by several developments. We outline four, which are of great importance for child theology and the role of the teacher.

A first development is that of pluralization. Dutch society, as many western societies, has a great and increasing diversity of worldview beliefs.[1] This diversity is not only recognizable throughout society, but certainly also in school teams and student populations.[2] Therefore it is not surprising that some academic researchers plead for embracing the variety of religious and secular views by replacing the concept of religious education with the concept of worldview education.[3] The diversity of worldview beliefs is reflected in the tightened Citizenship Law for primary and secondary education[4] which states that schools need to focus on "teaching knowledge about and respect for differences." There is also the pluralization of society in terms of sexual and gender identity and cultural backgrounds.

Second, we see a de-pillarization in society as a whole and thus also in Dutch education.[5] Established religious traditions have lost their authority for many people.[6] Educational professionals are often driven by motivations linked to a deep sense of meaning, without that sense of meaning belonging to a particular religious or worldview tradition.[7] But with the loss of this authority, religion and worldview have not disappeared from the scene. Religion has been transformed.[8] Philosophy of life and searching for meaning have become individual processes that increasingly take place independently of institutions and traditions. The construction of identity and meaning has become an individual quest:[9] people in a Western society such as the Dutch bricolage their own worldview values and form their "patchwork identity."[10] We see this as a process of individualization in which individual choices and values are paramount.[11]

1 Moyaert, "Inter-worldview"; Miedema and Avest, "In the Flow."
2 Milot, "Religious Dimension."
3 Valk, Selçuk, and Miedema, "Worldview."
4 VO-raad, *Burgerschapsonderwijs*.
5 Avest, Bakker, Bertram-Troost, and Miedema, "Religion."
6 Mulder and Van den Berg, "Learning."
7 Mulder, "Werken."
8 Kalsky, "Inleiding."
9 Kalsky, "Inleiding."
10 Mulder, "Werken," 29.
11 Mulder, "Werken."

A third development concerns the growing phenomenon of cooperation schools.[12] These are a relatively new phenomenon in the Dutch educational system. Cooperation schools are the result of a merger between one (or more) public school and one (or more) school for non-government, denominational education. The characteristics specific to each original school come together in a new type of school. This increases the diversity of the student population: teachers, students, and certainly parents with a preference for public education form a new school with teachers, parents, and students who have affinity with denominational education. Thus, in education (mostly) religious values come together with secular values. An important goal here is to find a connecting story that is value based and that guides denominational and public education. The phenomenon of the cooperation school points to a deeper development: the identity, the values of public and denominational education are developing towards each other and both "types" of schools are to a large extent no longer exclusively recognizable by their ideological values.[13]

Finally, we point to the increasing religious illiteracy of students and also of teachers.[14] Knowledge of and familiarity with worldview (and therefore religious) sources is declining. This development explicitly presents the worldview education of students with the question whether and how this education can connect to and make use of worldview traditions when these may be assumed to be less and less familiar.[15]

What opportunities and dilemmas do these developments present to child theology, especially in education? And what is then required of the teacher? In this article we explore child theology from a hermeneutic-communicative perspective. We focus in particular on the tasks expected of a teacher, especially in the context of the described developments, in worldview education in primary and secondary schools. Here we have in mind both denominational and public education, young children and older teenagers.

12 Renkema, *Two*.

13 Zoontjens, *Weg*.

14 Valk, Selçuk, and Miedema, "Worldview Literacy."

15 Roebben, *Inclusieve godsdienstpedagogiek*.

Child Theology and a Hermeneutical-Communicative Perspective

Based on insights from Schweitzer,[16] Valstar and Kuindersma distinguish three activities as the core of child theology: theologizing from children, theologizing with children and theologizing for children.[17]

Given the focus of this article, we will suffice to emphasize that child theology, and these three activities as its essential features, aims at bringing children's experiences and perspectives into dialogue with those of (other) young and adult interlocutors and with incentives from worldview sources.[18] In doing so, we stimulate a curious, critical attitude toward one's own beliefs, those of another, and those from sources and traditions.[19] Ultimately, this attitude serves and is conditional for "the construction of their own faith story."[20]

The purpose of this article is to clarify which teacher roles are appropriate and necessary for children's theology. We bring in a hermeneutic-communicative perspective on worldview education. This is because we recognize similarities between this perspective and children's theology and because it enables us to shed more light on the roles and requirements of teachers. The hermeneutic-communicative perspective can shed light on the tasks of worldview education in the midst of the developments outlined, on the three activities of child theology, and on desirable roles of the teacher to foster the child's worldview development.

A hermeneutic-communicative perspective on worldview education is fundamentally premised on students growing up in a diverse society and on the value of diversity of sources and traditions (religious and secular) for student development.[21]

This also makes this perspective speak of worldview education and not exclusively religious education: thus, both religious and secular traditions and sources are valuable. The roles of a teacher also take that diversity of sources and traditions and in society as a crucial starting point. The goal of worldview education from the hermeneutic-communicative perspective is

16 Schweitzer, "Kindertheologie."
17 Valstar, "Quest."
18 Valstar, "Quest."
19 Dillen, "Theologizing."
20 Valstar and Kuindersma, *Verwonderen*, 146.
21 Mulder and Van den Berg, "Learning."

> not only and not foremost the transmission of meaningful information but particularly the construction of meaning in interaction: interactions with sources of meaning and interaction between students and teachers.[22]

We already see something of the teacher's roles illuminated in the description of both the hermeneutic and communicative dimensions of this perspective.

The hermeneutic dimension of worldview education requires the teacher to connect possible interpretations of worldview traditions and sources to students' perspectives, experiences and beliefs. The sources of meaning are crucial tools for using that connection to invite students to enter into conversation with those sources, to engage them critically, constructively and curiously. As an extension of the "construction of their own faith story"[23] mentioned above, Pollefeyt describes that in hermeneutic learning, a learner

> finds himself [herself] more deeply, more consciously, more complexly back in his or her own worldview story and learns to know and understand the other with discernment in his or her hermeneutic circle.[24]

The value of the communicative dimension of this approach lies in the teacher's ability to stimulate dialogue between students, the teacher and sources.[25] Fundamental to this is both "a commitment to an open and dialogical or 'conversational' religious education"[26] and the view that the teacher does not provide students with answers or lead them to them, but is one of the interlocutors and facilitates and encourages dialogue on worldview themes.[27]

Teachers' Viewpoints in Child Theology

A hermeneutic communicative approach to worldview education and thus to child theology focuses on three goals.[28] These goals are highly influenced by the developments mentioned in Section 1. To those goals we attach basic attitudes and fundamental viewpoints of the teacher. The goals and the

22 Mulder and Van den Berg, "Learning," 289.
23 Valstar and Kuindersma, *Verwonderen*, 146.
24 Pollefeyt, *Hermeneutisch leren*, 191.
25 Mulder and Van den Berg, "Learning."
26 Jackson, *Religious Education*, 135.
27 Heimbrock, "Encounter."
28 Mulder and Van den Berg, *Learning*.

viewpoints of teachers, as described in this section, form the foundation of the teacher roles described in Section 4.

The first goal of the hermeneutic communicative perspective on worldview education is the child's self-understanding, being able and allowed to express personal experiences, perspectives and questions. The student is invited to do so, challenged by an inquisitive and engaged teacher, and receives the space to contribute with original, divergent, but above all his or her own ideas. In the process of interaction with others and with sources, the teacher thereby stimulates the student also to scrutinize, detect, critically question, adjust, or (re)agree with those personal beliefs.

In this goal of hermeneutic-communicative worldview education, the teacher is concerned with the development of the student as a human being. Education, and certainly worldview education, does not focus, at least not exclusively and dominantly, on the cognitive transmission and mastery of subject matter or religious doctrines. Thereby, theologizing (and philosophizing) with, for and from children is grounded in the belief that children's vision and experiences are valuable to the process of development, in dialogue with others and with sources.[29] Teachers contribute to worldview development with an eye for the student as a human being, for contents and experiences that go beyond, deeper than learning and cognitive outcomes.[30] This emphasis on the learner as a developing human being also has its implications for citizenship education. The encounter with others, in the context of diversity, invites each learner to enter into dialogue with his/her own values and experiences and at the same time to feel addressed on a personal and existential level by that other, in her/his otherness.[31]

The second goal of worldview education, from the hermeneutic-communicative perspective, focuses on the dialogical relationship to diversity. That diversity is present both in the group of students and in society. In the dynamics of dialogue, students discover and experience that people, near and far, can think about and believe in existential and moral matters accordingly, differently and that differences can sometimes clash. "Students can converse about these differences in a respectful way to be prepared to contribute constructively and peacefully to debates in a plural and diverse society."[32] This goal has a clear relationship with the Citizenship Educa-

29 Parlevliet, *Leren Theologiseren*; Roebben, *Inclusieve godsdienstpedagogiek*.

30 Bertram-Troost, *Menswording*.

31 Bruin, Elsenaar, and Renkema, *Levensbeschouwelijk*.

32 Mulder and Van den Berg, *Learning*, 290–91.

tion Act as mandated for schools by the Dutch government since 2006.[33] Citizenship education can thus be seen as an opportunity. An opportunity that contributes

> to the development of understanding for other people's choices, even if they are not yours and do not have to become yours. A school is a society in miniature, where tolerance and alienation, understanding and disapproval are practiced. Even when the school population seems homogeneous at first glance, of course all students are different. Sometimes things chafe and clash considerably in a school. This also means that the strange and unheard views are valuable. It encourages students to practice dealing with differences, democratic coexistence, and encounter and dialogue.[34]

From this goal, the teacher sees diversity in the group of students and in society as a valuable and powerful engine both for student development[35] and for practicing an understanding way of living together.[36]

The third goal of the hermeneutic-communicative perspective on worldview education is for students to become worldview literate. Through the exploratory and hermeneutic approach to sources from worldview traditions, from art and media, past and present, students become familiar with those sources.[37] This familiarity invites them to relate personally, critically, and receptively to the contents and thus to the questions of existence raised by the sources. This goal is essentially linked to the first two goals: the hermeneutic handling of sources and traditions makes the student reflect on his or her own existence and understanding of life.[38] In addition, this literacy contributes to learning to live together and thus to the citizenship formation of students:

> Knowledge and awareness of the various worldviews, both religious and secular, and how they impact self, others, and societies at large can lead to greater understanding of differences, so that focus can shift to tensions that become creative rather than divisive.[39]

33 VO-raad, *Burgerschapsonderwijs*.
34 Bruin, Elsenaar, and Renkema, *Levensbeschouwelijk*, 10.
35 Elias, "Philosophical."
36 Miedema and Avest, "In the Flow"; Keaten and Soukup, "Dialogue."
37 Roebben, *Inclusieve godsdienstpedagogiek*.
38 Parlevliet, *Leren*.
39 Valk, Selçuk, and Miedema, "Worldview Literacy," 365.

This means that the teacher works from the vision that worldview sources, of whatever origin, are valuable tools for developing students' self-understanding and understanding of another. This vision is based on the premise that those sources (can) set in motion and inspire reflection on one's own existence and the world and are therefore not museum pieces from times gone by.[40]

The teacher endorses the value of those sources and of existential, philosophical, and theological questions and themes in education. This is an essential appreciation that offers a counter voice to the current emphasis in education on cognitive, objective, and measurable knowledge content.[41] Also, the teacher must have knowledge of sources and traditions. This includes both religious sources and secular sources, sources past and present.[42] Especially in a time and society like the Dutch one, this knowledge is not (anymore) obvious for teachers.[43] In addition, and intertwined with this worldview literacy of teachers, it requires from the teacher a "hermeneutical sensitivity":[44] the skill to help unlock the meaning(s) of a source and let the student enter into a dialogue with it.[45]

We already mentioned possible implications of the hermeneutic-communicative perspective for a keen vision of students' citizenship education. Since the commitment in 2006 and certainly after the tightening of the law on citizenship education in 2021,[46] education professionals and scholars have been busy fleshing out this education. The publication of the core objectives for citizenship education in primary and secondary schools in 2024 arose from the need to give schools direction in this regard.[47]

Precisely because the hermeneutic-communicative perspective takes its starting point in the diversity in society and in worldview sources, it is a valuable perspective for the citizenship assignment of schools. We pay attention here to the connection between citizenship education and the hermeneutic-communicative perspective on worldview education, because citizenship education very explicitly sets the agenda of schools, government, and society. In addition, we hereby demonstrate that the focus on child theology, underscored by the hermeneutic-communicative

40 Valk, Selçuk, and Miedema, "Worldview Literacy."
41 Valk, Selçuk, and Miedema, "Worldview Literacy."
42 Valstar, *The Quest.*
43 Parlevliet, *Leren.*
44 Roebben, *Inclusieve godsdienstpedagogiek*, 52.
45 Valstar and Kuindersma, *Verwonderen.*
46 VO-raad, *Burgerschapsonderwijs.*
47 Rijksoverheid, *Kerndoelen.*

perspective, has added value for teachers who want to do work on citizenship education and thus on education that seeks to teach students to live together understandingly in diversity. Therefore, the roles we ascribe to teachers in Section 4 are certainly roles that enable the teacher to give powerful form and content to citizenship education. This means that the citizenship education of students, from the hermeneutic-communicative perspective and with attention to child theology, is coloured by worldviews. We thus call citizenship education "worldview citizenship education."[48] It is education aimed at the formation of young people, in the context of diversity, in society and in worldview sources.[49]

This connection between child theology, from the hermeneutic-communicative perspective, and students' worldview citizenship education has a number of consequences for the teacher. Those consequences have their effect in the teacher roles described below and for a powerful interpretation of citizenship education: worldview citizenship education.

The first consequence of the connection between child theology, from the hermeneutic-communicative perspective on the one hand, and students' worldview citizenship education on the other hand, is that diversity in the classroom and in society is fundamentally regarded as valuable for student development. Attention to the student's personal story presupposes the space that may and should be available for this story. Student development benefits from the encounter with that diversity. This is by definition a worldview view of diversity and inclusion: the belief that the other is fundamentally equal in her/his otherness. This means that the teacher contributes to "developing a respectful attitude toward others, enabling them to feel accepted as they are. It also involves learning to live without feeling under threat because of one's differences."[50]

Second, the hermeneutic-communicative perspective on worldview education in connection with citizenship education means that the teacher, and thus education, has in mind the formation of students as human beings. The encounter with diversity, in the school and in society, is an invitation for the student to bring himself, with his/her experiences and worldview, into the dialogue with other perspectives. But it also means that this encounter affects the human being behind the learner, in the formation of the person, in her/his way of life and worldview.[51]

48 Miedema, *Coming Out*, 370; Bruin, Elsenaar and Renkema, *Levensbeschouwelijk*.
49 Bertram-Troost and Miedema, *Bezield*.
50 Milot, "Religious Dimension," 17.
51 Rautionmaa and Kallioniemi, "Integrated."

Third, the hermeneutic-communicative perspective enriches citizenship education, and thus the role of the teacher, with the conviction that the encounter in the context of diversity benefits greatly from attention to existential, philosophical and theological questions and worldview sources in which they are expressed. These invite students to enter into the encounter around those issues and sources and thereby to get to know the other at the level of existential values and worldview. Both learning to live together with differences and the individual education of the student, and thus the worldview citizenship education, receive a powerful stimulus.[52]

Teacher's Roles in Worldview Education

When we view the above-mentioned goals and starting positions of child theology from a hermeneutic-communicative perspective as an approach to worldview education that is in the midst of the developments as outlined in Section 1, this makes the teacher a crucial factor. This does not only apply to the teacher trained as a theologian or religious scholar, who teaches the subject of "Worldview" in secondary school. It applies to all teachers: the primary school teacher and the secondary school teacher of any subject. All have an essential task in the worldview formation of students and the encouragement of child theology.

To work on this and achieve the goals, the teacher must master several roles. We distinguish five roles that do justice to the above perspectives and developments and thus contribute to (the further development of) child theology. These roles thus focus on an appreciative handling of diversity in the student group and in society, underline the personal search for meaning of young people, tell a connecting story for denominational and public education and stimulate the worldview literacy of students (and teachers). We bring together the initial letters of these roles with the abbreviation TIMES.

Translator

First, the teacher is a *Translator*: she/he can translate worldview sources into life experiences that are both recognizable and surprising to students: educating with and about worldview sources challenges the teacher to

52 Valk, Selçuk, and Miedema, "Worldview Literacy."

translate them into questions and insights that strengthens students' views and experiences, but that also provides students with new perspectives.

This role does not require the teacher to have a personal connection to a source or tradition as existential truth. This role does not necessarily require the teacher to adhere to tradition. But the role of Translator does require the conviction that a source and a tradition, any one, is valuable to encounter critically and curiously and is hermeneutically significant for personal identity development.[53] This makes the teacher a professional who recognizes hermeneutical nodes in those sources, brings those sources into the learning process as valuable input for student development and dialogue, and can make the substantive connection to students' life questions and experiences. The teacher can ask questions that do justice to both the source and the students' perspectives and questions. Thus, pointing to the reality and questions of existence that are unlocked from the source.[54]

To perform the role of Translator, it is necessary for the teacher to be a specialist who knows his/her way in the world of worldview sources and traditions.[55] We recognize this role in the theory of child theology in which the teacher provides input in theologizing for children.[56]

Imaginator

The second role of the teacher is that of the *Imaginator*:[57] the teacher introduces students to symbolically charged images in worldview sources. Many of the religious and secular sources use imagination and symbolism to tell a story about life and the world. The teacher introduces students to this unique feature of worldview sources. Without this task, the sources are not done justice and a hermeneutic understanding is not possible.

In addition, the teacher knows how to develop in the student a "metaphoric sensitivity, inventive imagination, and creative interpretation."[58] When a student herself is invited to use imagination in reflecting on her own existence, she is addressed more than on a cognitive level. Therefore, the teacher challenges the learner to express the source and a life experience

53 Meijer, "Plural Selves."

54 Muynck and Kunz, *Gidsen.*

55 Pollefeyt, "Hermeneutisch"; Roebben, *Inclusieve godsdienstpedagogiek.*

56 Valstar, "Quest."

57 Mulder and Van den Berg, "Learning."

58 Mulder and Van den Berg, "Learning," 292.

in creative and personal images. For the latter, consider imagination in expressive paintings, drama forms or musical sounds, for example.

Moderator

Third, the teacher is a *Moderator*.[59] In guiding dialogizing and philosophizing, she/he connects students to each other. The teacher bears the responsibility that each student feels heard and challenged to express him/herself and respond to another with an open and curious mind. With this role, the teacher is at the heart of diversity where he/she is committed to "interaction between people socialised in different ways, having different opinions and different interests."[60] Here it is important to emphasize that diversity characterizes each group of students: each student represents a unique view, even if the group appears to be fairly homogeneous in worldview terms.[61]

In his/her role as moderator, the teacher is no longer the designated person who guides students toward answers. Rather, she/he becomes one of the participants and functions as a facilitator for the dialogue.[62] In the dialogue, the Moderator always has two dimensions in mind: the respectful connection between the students themselves and with any other interlocutors and, in addition, the development of the identity of the individual student. The latter means that the teacher must moderate in such a way that the student feels both safe enough and challenged to express himself in the dialogue.

We also recognize this role in the theory of theologizing with children: the theological dialogue among students makes the teacher a curious and alert connector.[63]

Explorer

The fourth role is that of the *Explorer*. The teacher explores the world of worldview traditions, of art and media, in the past and the present and that of the students. He/she does this by asking those questions that do

59 Mulder and Van den Berg, "Learning."
60 Meijer, "Plural Selves," 325.
61 Milot, "Religious Dimension."
62 Heimbrock, "Encounter."
63 Valstar, "Quest."

justice to both the source and the students' answers and experiences. In doing so, the teacher masters the art of questioning. She/he does this from the conviction that "personal identity [...] is necessarily tentative, to be reflected upon, reconsidered and revised again and again."[64] The teacher is curious for answers, for new questions, and challenges students to come up with their personal questions.[65]

Source

Finally, the teacher is a *Source*. The students, in addition to each other and worldview sources, also meet the teacher as he/she brings in personal values, motivations and existential questions. He/she never does this to convey a worldview, but to stimulate the students' search with a complementary perspective. With this, (worldview) education in general and the teacher in particular is by definition not neutral. In the pedagogical and didactic choices he/she makes, in the themes he/she raises, the questions he/she asks, his/her visions of good life and education are expressed.[66] But on top of that, the teacher also brings in his/her worldview visions and experiences as a resource from which students can learn,[67] not to adopt the teacher's input, but to sharpen their personal questions and insights. Sometimes a student may embrace a completely different perspective. In doing so, the teacher asks exploring questions and connects the student to others. In that dialogic connection, the teacher herself participates from a personal perspective on existence and worldview.

Conclusion

In child theology and worldview education in schools, the teacher is playing a crucial role. He/she is in the midst of challenging developments that demand much of his/her professionalism. In this article we have outlined five roles for teachers who want to contribute to child theology from the hermeneutic-communicative perspective. It is a challenging point of view for teachers, both in primary and in secondary education, teachers trained

64 Meijer, "Plural Selves," 325.
65 Roebben, *Inclusieve godsdienstpedagogiek*.
66 Muynck and Kunz, *Gidsen*.
67 Loobuyck, *Meer LEF*.

as a theologian or religious scholar, teachers of any subject at secondary school, teachers at primary school. Because of this challenging character of these roles, it requires vigorous training of new teachers and continuous professionalisation of teachers. Teachers' training must include a significant attention for the attitude, the knowledge and the skills of teachers. This training therefore starts with underlining a deepening vision of education in general and the worldview formation of students in particular: education is so much more than the transmission and measurement of knowledge. Beyond that, and including the acquisition of knowledge, education is aiming at the development of the student as a human being who is aware, dynamically and constructively, of experiences, lifestyles and beliefs that give her/him meaning to life and the world. The student does so in relation to another, near or far, physically, digitally or interpreted in a worldview source. This relationship constructs personal meaning and certainly (learning to) live together with differences. The school is there for people and society. The teacher can make an indispensable contribution to it.

Bibliography

Avest, Ina ter, Cok Bakker, Gerdien Bertram-Troost, and Siebren Miedema. "Religion and education in the Dutch pillarized and post-pillarized educational system. Historical background and current debates." In *Religion and Education in Europe. Developments, Contexts and Debates*, edited by R. Jackson et al. Münster: Waxmann, 2007, 203–19.

Bertram-Troost, Gerdien. *Menswording in een laag-vertrouwensamenleving. Kansen en uitdagingen voor onderwijs*. Amsterdam: Vrije Universiteit, 2022.

Bertram-Troost, Gerdien, and Siebren Miedema. *Bezield Onderwijs*. Gorredijk: Noordboek, 2022.

Bruin, Guido de, Marcel Elsenaar, and Erik Renkema. *Levensbeschouwelijk burgerschapsonderwijs. Werken aan burgerschap vanuit identiteit en pedagogische bedoeling*. Woerden: Verus, 2022.

Dillen, Annemie. "Theologizing With Children. A New Paradigm for Catholic Religious Education in Belgium and New Challenges for Catholic Schools." In *International Handbook of Catholic Education*, edited by G. Grace and J. O'Keefe. Vol. 2 of *International Handbooks of Religion and Education*. New York: Springer, 2007, 347–66.

Elias, John L. "Philosophical Reflections on Dialogue." In *International Handbook of Inter-religious Education. Part One*, edited by K. Engebretson , M. de Souza, G. Durka, and L. Gearon. New York: Springer, 2010, 57–72.

Heimbrock, Hans-Günter. "Encounter as Model for Dialogue in Religious Education." In *Religious Education as Encounter. A Tribute to John M. Hull*, edited by S. Miedema. Münster: Waxmann, 2009, 83–97.

Jackson, Robert. "Religious and Cultural Diversity. Some Key Concepts." In *Religious Diversity and Intercultural Education. A Reference Book for Schools*, edited by J. Keast. Council of Europe, 2006, 21–29.

Jackson, Robert. *Religious Education. An Interpretive Approach*. London: Hodder & Stoughton, 1997.

Kalsky, Manuela "Inleiding." In *Alsof ik thuis ben. Samenleven in een land vol verschillen*, edited by M. Kalsky. Almere: Parthenon, 2013, 11–31.

Keaten, James A., and Charles Soukup. "Dialogue and Religious Otherness. Toward a Model of Pluralistic Interfaith Dialogue." *Journal of International and Intercultural Communication* 2:2 (2009): 168–87.

Loobuyck, Patrick. *Meer LEF in het onderwijs. Levensbeschouwing, Ethiek en Filosofie voor iedereen*. Brussel: VUB-Press, 2014.

Meijer, Wilna A.J. "Plural Selves and Living Traditions. A Hermeneutical View on Identity and Diversity, Tradition and Historicity." In *International Handbook of the Religious, Moral and Spiritual Dimensions in Education*, edited by M. de Souza, K. Engebretson, G. Durka, R. Jackson, and A. McGrady. Vol. 1 of *International Handbooks of Religion and Education*. New York: Springer, 2009, 321–32.

Miedema, Siebren. "Coming Out Religiously! Religion, The Public Sphere, and Religious Identity Formation." *Religious Education* 109:34 (2014): 370.

Miedema, Siebren, and Ina ter Avest. "In the Flow to Maximal Interreligious Citizenship Education." *Religious Education* 106:4 (2011): 410–24.

Milot, Micheline. "The Religious Dimension in Intercultural Education." In *Religious Diversity and Intercultural Education. A Reference Book for Schools*, edited by J. Keast. Council of Europe, 2006, 13–20.

Marianne Moyaert. "Inter-worldview education and the re-production of good religion." *Education Sciences* 8:4 (2018): 1–15.

Mulder, André. "Werken met diepgang. Een introductie." In *Werken met diepgang*, edited by A. Mulder and H. Snoek. Zoetermeer: Meinema, 2012, 15–45.

Mulder, André, and Bas van den Berg "Learning for Life. A Hermeneutical–Communicative Model for Worldview Education and White Normativity." *Religious Education* 114:3 (2019): 287–302.

Mulder, André and Bas van den Berg. *Learning for Life. An Imaginative Approach to Worldview Education in the Context of Diversity*. Eugene: Wipf & Stock, 2019.

Muynck, Bram de, and Bram Kunz. *Gidsen. Een christelijke schoolpedagogiek*. Utrecht: KokBoekencentrum, 2021.

Parlevliet, Leendert-Jan. *Leren Theologiseren met kinderen, Leerkrachten van een basisschool en een perspectiefwisseling in het godsdienstonderwijs*. Vlissingen: HZ University of Applied Sciences, 2017.

Pollefeyt, Didier "Hermeneutisch leren in het vak godsdienst." In *Handboek Vakdidactiek Levensbeschouwing & Religie. Leven Leren vanuit je Wortels*, edited by M. van Dijk-Groeneboer et al. Expertisecentrum Levensbeschouwing en Religie in het Voortgezet Onderwijs, 2020, 187–200.

Rautionmaa, Heidi, and Arto Kallioniemi. "Integrated Religious Education to Promote Dialogue in Inter-worldview Education." In *Interfaith Education for All. Theoretical Perspectives and Best Practices for Transformative Action*, edited by D. Wielzen and Ina ter Avest. Rotterdam: Sense Publishers, 2017, 147–158.

Renkema, Erik. *Two Of A Kind. The Identity Of Cooperation Schools In The Netherlands And The Correlation With Religious Education*. Ede: GVO, 2018.

Rijksoverheid. *Kerndoelen burgerschap* (2024). Accessed April 13, 2024. www.rijksoverheid.nl/documenten/rapporten/2024/03/06/conceptkerndoelen-burgerschap.

Roebben, Bert. *Inclusieve godsdienstpedagogiek. Grondlijnen voor levensbeschouwelijke vorming*. Leuven, Den Haag: Acco, 2015.

Schweitzer, Friedrich. "Was ist und wozu Kindertheologie?" In *Im Himmelreich ist keiner sauer. Kinder als Exegeten*, edited by A. A. Buchter et al. Stuttgart: Calwer, 2003, 9–18.

Valk, John, Mualla Selçuk, and Siebren Miedema. "Worldview Literacy in the Academy and Beyond. Advancing Mutual Understanding in Diverse Societies." *Religious Education* 115:3 (2020): 364–74.

Valstar, Johan. "The Quest for Powerful Learning Environments." In *Powerful Learning Environments and Theologizing and Philosophizing with Children*, edited by H. Kuindersma. Kassel: University Press GmbH, 2013, 14–30.

Valstar, Johan, and Henk Kuindersma *Verwonderen en ontdekken*. Amersfoort: NZV Uitgevers, 2008.

VO-raad. *Burgerschapsonderwijs*. Accessed April 13, 2024. www.vo-raad.nl/onderwerpen/burgerschapsonderwijs/wat-speelt-er,.

Zoontjens, Paul. *De weg naar burgerschap. Afscheidsrede Paul Zoontjens, als hoogleraar onderwijsrecht van Tilburg University*. Tilburg: Tilburg University, 2019.

Amsterdam University Press

YEARBOOK OF CONTEXTUAL BIBLICAL INTERPRETATION 1 (2024) 116-147
HTTPS://DOI.ORG/10.5117/YCBI2024.008.WEST

CBI as a (Biblical Studies) Discipline

Gerald O. West, Professor Emeritus in the School of Religion, Philosophy, and Classics in the University of KwaZulu-Natal, South Africa

Abstract

"Contextual Biblical Interpretation" (CBI) as a concept has been useful because of its broad and inclusive scope. The article identifies a number of conceptual parameters of CBI. First, CBI includes biblical studies work in which the context of biblical reception is the subject of interpretation. Second, the context of reception is an inhabited or peopled context and these actual local context-based people are the subjects of interpretation. Third, the different forms of CBI each include a commitment to forms of social and theological transformation. Fourth, the various forms of CBI, while accountable to reception context-based readers are each "biblical" in that they may use of the resources of biblical studies, while challenging and changing the discipline. Fifth, CBI contributes to the changing of the discipline of biblical studies through its careful conceptual work, creating communities of theoretical and methodological reflection within forms of action-reflection praxis.

Keywords: Contextual Biblical Interpretation, Contextual Bible Study, Intercultural biblical interpretation, context of reception, context of production, liberation

Introduction

"Contextual Biblical Interpretation" (CBI) as a concept has been useful because of its broad and inclusive scope. Various kinds of contextual biblical interpretation have found a place within the family resemblances of CBI. In this article I reflect further on the concept of CBI, offering both an analysis of the different kinds of contextual biblical interpretation that might constitute CBI and the beginning of an archive of such CBI work.

I have invoked the term "family resemblances" from the work of Ludwig Wittgenstein, recognizing that there is no one "essence" common to what we call CBI, and that it would be more useful to identify how various forms of contextual biblical interpretation "are *related* to one another in many different ways."[1] My purpose in the conceptual analysis is not to circumscribe and exclude, but to recognize resonances between related forms of contextual biblical interpretation. Indeed, I have tried to be as inclusive of CBI diversity as possible. My hope is that this article will encourage further conceptual reflection on CBI.

I have used both "Contextual Biblical Interpretation" (with upper case) and "contextual biblical interpretation" (with lower case) in order to signal that I am not assuming that the kinds of contextual biblical interpretation engaged with by the Centre for Contextual Biblical Interpretation (CCBI), who commissioned this article and who are the publishers of the *Yearbook for Contextual Biblical Interpretation*, are inclusive of the many related forms of contextual biblical interpretation. The use of the upper case term and the abbreviation tends to be limited to a Dutch context of reception, whereas other contexts of reception use other terms. CBI may come in time to be used as a superordinate designation for the related family of contextual biblical interpretation practice in various contexts, and this *Yearbook for Contextual Biblical Interpretation* may play a conceptual and archival role in a broader acceptance of this formulation.

My use of the abbreviation "CBI" in this article is inclusive of "Contextual Biblical Interpretation" in the Dutch sense and of "contextual biblical interpretation" as it is used more widely. I have already indicated where I think we should begin in our understanding of CBI. A common feature of any and every form of CBI, I would suggest, is that the reception context of biblical interpretation is the *subject* of biblical interpretation.

Reception context as the subject of biblical interpretation

My own contextual bias is evident here, for I refer in this formulation to what has become a classic African understanding of CBI: "the people's context becomes the *subject* of interpretation of the biblical text."[2] Our colleague, the late Justin Ukpong, is referring specifically to African biblical interpretation, but his conceptual formulation offers a starting point, I would argue, for all

1 Wittgenstein, *Philosophical*, § 67, 65.

2 Ukpong, "Developments," 24.

CBI. CBI has as its core hermeneutical identity the context of the readers, hearers, and users of the Bible.

In this sense CBI is orientated to the reception vector of South African Bernard Lategan's incisive characterization of the different hermeneutical approaches within biblical studies. In Lategan's conceptual analysis of biblical hermeneutics, biblical studies as a discipline has developed historically from an emphasis on the socio-historical dimensions of biblical text production, to a recognition of the synchronic dimensions of the biblical text as literary-narrative "text," to an often reluctant acknowledgement by the biblical studies guild of the role of an actual real reader.[3] Ukpong reverses this ordering, recognizing the reality that African biblical interpretation begins with the African readers, hearers, users of the Bible. The other hermeneutical vectors are not ignored, they are just not the starting point.

Both Lategan and Ukpong offer their analysis from the perspective of what today would be considered postcolonial criticism, but neither of them use this term. Lategan uses the notion of "social transformation" and Ukpong uses the notion of "inculturation hermeneutics," but both recognize that their dialogue partner is "Western" understandings of biblical studies. Each has much more to say about the priority of the context of the reader, but for now my point is simply to note that in their analysis African and Third World forms of biblical interpretation are "contextual" forms of biblical interpretation precisely because in these forms of biblical interpretation the people's context has become the *subject* of interpretation of the biblical text.

In my introduction to this article I indicated that my focus is both conceptual and archival. While there is not the space in the article for comprehensive documentation of CBI, my article is an attempt to document key examples of the kinds of family forms of CBI that constitute CBI. It is for this reason that I have cited the particular versions of Ukpong's and Lategan's publications, though each of them has published these articles in more than one form. I have chosen citation sites which offer an array of other related scholarship so that the reader of my article might follow more recent related CBI reflection within collated collections. In the case of Ukpong's article, I have chosen the version published in one of the early edited compilations of African biblical scholarship, within which each essay offers a form of CBI, for in each the African context is the subject of biblical interpretation. In the case of Lategan, I have chosen a version published in

3 Lategan, "Current," 15–16.

an edited collection of his essays, each of which wrestle with contextual biblical hermeneutical analysis.

As is already evident in my conceptual analysis, an emphasis on context is also an emphasis on those who people this context. CBI is an embodied interpretive process. In the next section I elaborate on the reader, hearer, user of the Bible.

The subjects of the context of reception are the subjects of interpretation

CBI places considerable emphasis on actual real readers, hearers, and users of the Bible. This includes biblical scholars,[4] but is never restricted to biblical scholars. Indeed, pivotal to CBI is a substantive interpretive place for the non-scholarly reader, to use the term preferred by Teresa Okure.[5] My own preference has been the term "the ordinary reader," in which I am specific about how I use the term, referring in general to any reader, hearer, user of the Bible who is not a biblical scholar, and referring specifically to poor and marginalized readers, hearers, users of the Bible.[6] In the work of the Institute for the Study of the Bible (ISB), which became the Institute for the Study of the Bible and Worker Ministry Project (ISB Worker Ministry), which has become the Ujamaa Centre for Community Development and Research (Ujamaa Centre), the ordinary poor and marginalized reader (as a reader, hearer, user) of the Bible is epistemologically privileged, in line with the emphasis on epistemology which characterised the analysis of the Ecumenical Association of Third World Theologians (EATWOT), an organization of theologians from Asia, Africa, Latin America, and the margins of the First World (including African American Black Theology).[7]

Pioneering work in this regard, which has shaped the work of the Ujamaa Centre and CBI generally, has been the community-context-based work of Centro de Estudios Biblicos (CEBI) in Brazil, known as "the Popular Reading

4 Wit and West, eds., *African*.

5 Okure, "Feminist," 77.

6 West, *Biblical Hermeneutics*, 174–200.

7 Frostin, *Liberation Theology*, 3–4. This version is available electronically from the Ujamaa Centre, in collaboration with the Per Frostin Foundation. The bibliography remains one of the most comprehensive in terms of liberation theologies. See specifically Appiah-Kobi and Torres. eds., *African*; Fabella and Torres, eds., *Irruption*; Fabella and Oduyoye, eds., *With Passion*; Fabella and Torres, eds., *Doing Theology*.

of the Bible." In a useful methodological and historical overview of CEBI, Edmilson Schinelo collates decades worth of action and reflection.[8] In the Appendix at the end of his resource, Schinelo and others offer us "a brief history, not of CEBI as a whole, but of some moments in which the theme of methodology was given more emphasis."[9] CEBI-like work begins in late 1977, with the concern

> to accompany, with care and through the eyes of faith, what was happening to the people. One of the things which was most strongly felt was the appetite of the popular communities for the Word of God and the urgent need to nourish them.[10]

From this concern

> CEBI was born. It was born from a very concrete need, felt by many people for many years, to articulate a service which would help people from the Ecclesiastical Communities in the use and interpretation of the Bible.[11]

Central to CBI is the interpretive presence of "the people," particularly the poor and marginalized. But what is the role of the people in contextual biblical interpretation? The early emphasis of CEBI's work, as well as the emphasis in other related forms of contextual biblical interpretation, was on "biblical updating or rereading,"[12] whereby socially-engaged biblical scholars accompanied the people and deepened their understanding of the socio-historical dimensions of the Bible. Though the interpretive impetus was from the socially-engaged scholar to the ordinary reader, what provided methodological coherence to this direction was that it was understood that "the Bible was 'the memory of the poor'; it was considered as coming totally from below, from the experience of the destitute, where God dwells."[13] Néstor Míguez elaborates on this connection between the Bible's history and the people's history:

8 Schinelo, ed., *The Bible*.
9 Schinelo ed., *The Bible*, 6.
10 Schinelo ed., *The Bible*, 57.
11 Schinelo ed., *The Bible*, 57.
12 Schinelo ed., *The Bible*, 58.
13 Míguez, "Latin American," 128.

> The Bible was entirely the 'book of the people', ideologically captured by the powerful and conquerors, but now the poor and powerless were recovering their own heritage, and bringing back the true meaning of the text.[14]

In order for the people to understand the Bible as the book of the people socially engaged biblical scholars served the people by explaining biblical history as an analogical form of their own story of struggle.

The context of the people was foregrounded and the subjectivity of the people was affirmed. However, in these early forms of CBI the socially engaged biblical scholar played a significant role in re-reading the Bible, given the emphasis on socio-historical reconstruction of the biblical story of liberation. In a substantive sense the Bible was being re-read on behalf of the people. Much of the published work of CEBI over more than forty years does this,[15] as does work published in the journal *Revista de Interpretacion Biblica Latinoamericana*,[16] as does much of the early work of the ISB.[17]

The later work of the ISB, now the Ujamaa Centre, as well as various regional sites of CEBI's work, shifted the focus from re-reading the Bible on behalf of the people to re-reading the Bible *with* the people. The emphasis on the preposition "with" is deliberate and has been the focus of decades of conceptual reflection.[18] The Ujamaa Centre's form of CBI, "Contextual Bible Study" (CBS), pivots on participatory ways of re-reading the Bible in which organized formations of ordinary readers and socially engaged biblical scholars from the Ujamaa Centre interpret together: with each other. While our methodological reflections offer extensive analysis of our CBS praxis,[19] it is our various CBS "manuals" which have been summoned and produced from our praxis (many of which have included collaboration with CEBI practitioners) that perhaps best show how CBS reads *with*.[20] The socially engaged biblical scholar plays a significant role in the design of each CBS, but the actual re-reading interpretive process is controlled by the community-based facilitator. Even within our research publications

14 Míguez, "Latin American," 128.

15 https://cebi.org.br (accessed April 19, 2024).

16 For a selection of articles translated into English see Vaage, ed., *Subversive*.

17 Nürnberger, ed., *I will send*; Wittenberg, *I have heard*; Wittenberg, *Prophecy*; Wittenberg, *Resistance*; West, "Contextual Bible Study as a form of contextual theology."

18 West and Dube, eds., *Reading with*; Ukpong, "Bible"; West, ed., *Reading Other-Wise*.

19 West, "Reading the Bible"; West and Zwane, "Re-reading."

20 I cite here the Ujamaa "manual", but see also the list of related manuals below in footnote 96: Ujamaa, *Doing*.

we have become more overt about the dynamics of the "reading with" process.[21]

However, alongside this emphasis on an egalitarian interpretive facilitation praxis, there remains the concern evident in both CEBI's and the ISB's early work for the conscientizing role of the socially engaged biblical scholar, with respect to both the complex reality of the biblical text and the complex reality of the receptor context. This remains an aspect of the CBI process in which there are differences among biblical studies practitioners.[22]

Early CBI understandings of the Bible as "the book of the people," Míguez notes, gradually shifted. The hermeneutic of trust in the Bible evident in early forms of liberation theology shifted in the 1990s, even in Latin American Liberation Theology. "It took a certain time," explains Míguez, "and specially the critique of feminist hermeneutics, to realize that, even though that was true in great measure, it could not be affirmed without certain caveats."[23] He elaborates, using an analysis very similar to that of South African Itumeleng Mosala,[24] saying,

> the Bible was a more complex memory, with diverse trajectories in itself, with internal diversity and even contradictions. The memories had been reshaped in different hands and generations; scribes that wrote the people's traditions were not innocent and without their own vested interests, and the patriachalism of the culture became inscribed in the text. Thus, the hegemonic function of religion and the biases inscribed in popular culture, previously ignored, turned to be more evident.[25]

A crucial feature of the Ujamaa Centre's CBS methodology from the very beginning was the recognition from within South African Black Theology that the Bible was intrinsically a site of struggle and contestation,[26] primarily in terms of economics and class, but also in terms of gender.[27] It is not only biblical interpretation that is the problem but the Bible itself. Within each and every text there are contending ideological and

21 West, Zwane, and Van der Walt, "From Homosexuality."

22 Nadar, "Beyond"; Nadar, "Hermeneutics."

23 Míguez, "Latin American," 8.

24 Mosala, "The Use."

25 Míguez, "Latin American," 8.

26 Mosala, *Biblical.*

27 Mosala, *Biblical.*

theological voices. The Ujamaa Centre works with this understanding of the Bible, whether implicitly or explicitly.[28]

Turning from ambiguous realities of the biblical text to the ambiguous realities of "the people," Míguez continues:

> what is "popular" had to be redefined. The ambiguity of 'culture' called for a more careful and close vigilance of the prejudices, inequalities, bias and concealed interests in the Bible itself as well as in the readers, even the 'poor and simple'. Different situations of diverse 'subjects' (African descendants, aboriginal peoples, mestizos, women, campesinos, etc., and the crisscrossing of these categories) showed that there is no 'simple poor', but a complexity of reading locations that could not be ignored.[29]

In sum, Míguez says,

> a liberating interpretation of Scriptures could not be fundamentalist of any one given location, or naïve in its appropriation of the text. A liberationist hermeneutics must also be self-critical, give account of the complexities and contradictions within the text as well as in the reading community.[30]

I have cited Míguez extensively because he offers us an insightful analysis of where liberationist forms of CBI across the Global South find themselves today.

Much of early CBI work from the 1970s has been "political-economic" in its orientation and can be located within a liberation paradigm.[31] This would include the "cultural" orientation of most African contextual biblical interpretation, given the postcolonial and even decolonial perspective of those forms of CBI.[32] However, various appropriations by the margins of our world of the CBS work of the Ujamaa Centre, for example, have taken other directions, including sex work, liturgical-theological work, mental health work, and health and healing work.[33]

28 West, Zwane, and Van der Walt, "Resisting."

29 Míguez, "Latin American," 8–9.

30 Míguez, "Latin American," 9.

31 See for example Yong-Bock, *A Report*; Schinelo, *The Bible.*

32 Ngwa, *Let My People Live*; Mbuvi, *African.*

33 Ipsen, *Sex working*; Riches et al., *What is Contextual Bible Study?*; Mainwaring, *Mark*; Makoka and West, *Health-promoting.*

A related but distinctive cultural form of CBI emerged in our new millennium, drawing together both those who were doing liberationist CBI work and those engaged in empirical forms of CBI work. "Intercultural biblical interpretation" shares many family resemblances with its more political-economic sister form of CBI, and I offer this mode of CBI considerable space in this article because of its association with the work of the CCBI. Historically, many of those who were invited to be a part of the inaugural intercultural biblical interpretation project were active with liberationist forms of CBI, as the list of contributors and their contributions demonstrates in the inaugural collected volume.[34] Locating intercultural biblical hermeneutics alongside or even within political forms of CBI is not a strange thing to do, for intercultural biblical hermeneutics locates itself within this trajectory.

As Hans de Wit, one of its key theoreticians and practitioners, has argued,

> [i]ntercultural hermeneutics attempts to bring the inculturation of biblical stories within one culture into relationship with their inculturation in another context, not for the sake of intercultural discussion itself, but to make it serve the quest for truth, justice, and life. For this reason, we speak about intercultural hermeneutics of liberation.[35]

But it is not just this claim that locates intercultural hermeneutics within the trajectory of liberationist CBI, it is the pivotal place that both context and dialogue have in its reading praxis. Recognising the Enlightenment's reluctance to embrace the contextual pole of the process of understanding, intercultural biblical hermeneutics too is rooted in 'the response to the text'; it too is rooted in contexts of reception.[36]

In delimiting the field of intercultural biblical hermeneutics De Wit begins with the notion that "texts do something with their readers," particularly sacred texts; "[r]eception, a response from the readers, is constitutive of the meaning of texts."[37] However, intercultural biblical hermeneutics goes further than most "genitive theologies,"[38] extending the range of interpretive dialogue partners. In addition to the liberationist emphasis on a dialogue

34 Wit et al., eds., *Through the eyes*.
35 Wit, "Intercultural hermeneutics," 487; Wit, *Empirical*, 11.
36 Wit, *Empirical*, 11.
37 Wit, *Empirical*, 9.
38 Wit, *Empirical*, 11, 20.

between socially engaged biblical scholars and ordinary socio-economically poor readers, intercultural CBI includes a host of other Bible readers. At the core of this form of CBI is an "inter-cultural" dialogue. The dialogical dimension includes empirically validated organised interaction and even confrontation across often radically different contexts of reception.[39] And while the "cultural" in "intercultural" often does denote an exchange across different cultures, De Wit uses the term "intercultural" as an ethical concept that implies and signifies "the other" (in Emmanuel Levinas' sense), where the concept of "cultural" is used "because of the fundamental meaning of culture in people's mental programming."[40] Intercultural biblical hermeneutics, argues De Wit,

> does not demand that genitive hermeneutics give up what belongs to its specificity, namely, the attention to the local situation. Rather, intercultural hermeneutics invites genitive hermeneutics to take a critical look at its expressions of exclusion.[41]

In other words, intercultural hermeneutics reminds liberationist contextual biblical interpretation of the presence of "other" "cultural" contextual contexts.

For intercultural biblical hermeneutics there is no privileged local context or community. The "infinity" of "the other," both in terms of the text's eschatological horizon and in the multiplicity of local contexts,[42] keeps the reading process open and incomplete. There is always another appropriation and another reading community. Yet the other is never vague, is always specific.[43] Through "empirical" reading-reports, an integral part of the intercultural Bible reading process,[44] we come to know the other and how this particular other reads.[45] While intercultural biblical hermeneutics has tended to include the poor and marginalized among its reading groups in each of its projects,[46] their presence is not necessary to any particular encounter between groups.

39 Wit, *Empirical*, 27
40 Wit, *Empirical*, 27; Wit, "Through the eyes," 25–29.
41 Wit, "Intercultural Hermeneutics," 481.
42 Wit, *Empirical*, 47–49.
43 Wit, *Empirical*, 49.
44 Wit, *Empirical*, 18.
45 Wit, *Empirical*, 27–32
46 See for example Wit and López, eds., *The Widow*.

The primary role of the socially engaged biblical scholar within intercultural biblical interpretation is to coordinate the empirical dimensions of the encounter between different cultural interpretive groups. The socially engaged biblical scholar has no other specific role within intercultural biblical interpretation, though the process does document what can and does happen "when ordinary and professional readers sit across from each other." [47] As with other forms of CBI in which ordinary readers occupy a pivotal role, within intercultural CBI there is a clear recognition that ordinary intercultural contextual interpretations offer a "gift" to the exegete, and can "orient" the exegete in their scholarly work.[48]

While intercultural biblical interpretation shares a socio-economic legacy with liberationist forms of CBI, its intercultural interpretive process allows for any significant contextual or textual feature to be distinctive for a particular reading group. Because the reading process is left open to each particular reading group, the life experience and interests that shape the biblical interpretation of any particular group that are brought to the text are diverse; no particular set of social factors or social systems are foregrounded. However, the sisterly relationship between intercultural and political-economic forms of CBI continues to find expression in the self-understanding of intercultural biblical interpretation: "The task of intercultural hermeneutics," argues De Wit, "is primarily to offer insight into the degree to which people are prisoners of dominant reading traditions."[49] By encountering how "the other" reads the same text, through organized intercultural engagement, readers within a particular cultural context are "extracted" from their dominant reading traditions.[50] Through the intercultural encounter the text is granted (an-other) chance to speak, in which "the text cracks dominant cultural, social, political, and religious codes in a radical and absolutely revelatory way."[51] This almost postcolonial[52] ideological and theological aspect of intercultural CBI has been foregrounded in some of the major collaborative intercultural CBI projects, including a project focussed on violence against women, "Rape and Outrage: Case Studies on 2 Samuel 13,"[53] and a project focussed on resisting political impunity,

47 Wit, *Empirical*, 71.
48 Wit, *Empirical*, 78, 72.
49 Wit, *Empirical*, 46.
50 Wit, *Empirical*, 64.
51 Wit, *Empirical*, 65.
52 Segovia, "Reading-across."
53 Wit and Dyk, eds., *Bible and transformation*, 143–257.

"Intercultural Reading of Luke 18:1-8 in Latin American Contexts of Impunity."[54]

In each of these edited collections of essays there is extensive detailed reflection on intercultural CBI as a methodology. Like its liberationist sister, whether the work of CEBI or the Ujamaa Centre or related work from other contexts, intercultural biblical interpretation has an extensive conceptual bibliography, including the relationship between this form of CBI and other forms of CBI.[55] What these two intercultural biblical interpretation projects also demonstrate is how this form of CBI shares a concern about the relationship between biblical interpretation and social transformation.

Subjects of interpretation transforming their reception contexts through biblical interpretation

As indicated, intercultural CBI, like its political-economic sister forms of CBI, is concerned about transformation. Organised (intercultural) encounters between reception contexts produces forms of transformation, and intercultural hermeneutics attempts to document and analyse the nature of this transformation. Indeed, one of the objectives of this method is to address what it sees as an inadequacy of liberationist forms of CBI, namely a more careful account of "whether the praxis of liberation is a product of the new, careful way of Bible reading, or whether the text is already held hostage by an existing praxis."[56] Intercultural biblical interpretation probes the relationship between Bible reading and social action/transformation, and asks what kinds of social action/transformation actually emerge from contextual biblical interpretation. De Wit notes that the empirical material gathered by the intercultural Bible reading project shows, in fact, very little praxis of the socio-political kind. Intercultural Bible study does not, the research shows, often lead directly into action.[57] But this does not mean, he argues, that forms of liberation are not present. They are, but they are found in "the small gesture,"[58] not the macro-systemic action envisioned by

54 Wit and López, *The Widow*.

55 Segovia, "Reading-across"; Schipani, Brinkman, and Snoek, eds., *New Perspectives*; West, "Locating 'Contextual Bible Study'"; López, "Contextual Bible reading and intercultural Bible reading."

56 Wit, *Empirical*, 63.

57 Wit, *Empirical*, 63.

58 Wit, *Empirical*, 65.

liberation praxis; though, he acknowledges, the intercultural methodology might offer resources for development work.[59]

The relationship between CBI and participatory forms of community-based development has become increasingly the focus of the work of the Ujamaa Centre. While our CBS work has always been understood by our partners in community-based and church-based development projects as making a "transformative" contribution to their development agendas,[60] our recent research has become overt about accompanying and documenting the participatory community-based work of the local communities we work with.[61]

A distinctive feature of CBI is that CBI contributes towards contextual change. Though not all CBI work is overt about this dimension, the explicit or implicit engagement with a peopled context of reception in which the Bible is a significant text is suggestive of contextual change. Feminist biblical scholarship is a good example, even when this form of contextual biblical interpretation has no overt or actual local community-based interpretive partner. The pioneering literary-narrative work of Phyllis Trible not only offered ordinary readers a more egalitarian form of access to biblical scholarship than was evident with socio-historical methods, she also understood her work to offer resources for contextual change. Situating her feminist contextual biblical interpretation within "interactions between the Hebrew Scriptures and the Women's Liberation Movement,"[62] she offers "the depatriarchalizing principle" within scripture itself as a resource,[63] demonstrating "that the Hebrew Scriptures and Women's Liberation do meet and that their encounter need not be hostile."[64] Even biblical texts of terror, she demonstrates, "may yield new beginnings."[65] "In the speaking and the hearing" of these "sad stories," Trible says, "new things appear in the land."[66] She aligns her form of feminist CBI with feminism as "a prophetic movement," offering "a critique of culture and faith in light of misogyny [...], examining the status quo, pronouncing judgement, and calling for repentance."[67] This

59 Wit, *Empirical*, 85–6.
60 West and Ndlazi, "Leadership"; West, "Recovering."
61 Zwane, *Invited*; Zwane, "Ujamaa"; West, Zwane, and Carlos, "Contending."
62 Trible, "Depatriarchalization," 30.
63 Trible, "Depatriarchalization," 48.
64 Trible, "Depatriarchalization," 47.
65 Trible, *Texts*, 2.
66 Trible, *Texts*, 1.
67 Trible, *Texts*, 23.

kind of feminist biblical studies work, which has communities of women as indirect, at the very least, dialogue partners, and which imagines the contribution of biblical studies making a real contextual difference, forms a significant trajectory within feminist biblical studies and shares family resemblances with CBI.[68]

Most forms of contextual biblical interpretation summon contextual transformation, whether directly as in the work of CEBI and the Ujamaa Centre, or indirectly in the work of intercultural biblical interpretation and the host of scholarly forms of context of reception oriented biblical interpretation. Alongside feminist forms of CBI there has been a substantive body of Womanist and African Women's contextual biblical interpretation. Each of these forms of "feminist" biblical contextual interpretation have deliberately transgressed the boundary between the academy and the local contextual community of reception, precisely because they are forms of biblical scholarship which consider themselves to be about contextual change. However, because the "Biblical Studies" academy (with upper case) in the Euro-American zone remains ambivalent, at best, about overtly "contextual" CBI-type work, contributions to this trajectory of CBI scholarship foreground the "biblical" component rather than contemporary "contextual" change, though this is always present in some guise.[69]

The Third World "biblical studies" academy (with lower case) is less anxious about an overt contemporary contextual activist-development orientation, as the work of the Circle of Concerned African Women Theologians (the Circle) amply demonstrates in their many publications.[70] In the Third World, or Global South, the discipline of biblical studies has itself been transformed by forms of CBI. Here the people's context has become the subject of interpretation of the biblical text. African Biblical Studies[71] or African Biblical Interpretation[72] or African Biblical Hermeneutics[73] has already shifted the scholarly discipline of biblical studies towards the context of reception with its real actual local readers, hearers, and users of the Bible. A similar shift is taking place in the Asia-Pacific, with pioneering work in this respect being done by the Society of Asian Biblical Studies (SABS)

68 For a collection of essays inspired by Trible's work see Melanchthon and Whitaker, eds., *Terror*. See also Claassens, Maier, and Olojede, eds., *Transgression*; Claassens et al., eds., *Queering*.

69 See for example Weems, "Reading"; Byron and Lovelace, *Womanist interpretations*.

70 See for example Dube, ed., *Other Ways*; Dube and Kanyoro, eds., *Grant me*.

71 Mbuvi, "African."

72 Dube, Mbuvi, and Mbuwayesango, *Postcolonial*.

73 Masenya and Ngwa, eds., *Navigating*.

since 2006 (though work was begun in 1997), the Oceania Biblical Studies Association (since 2010), and Talanoa Oceania (since 2021).[74]

Indeed, what CBI has done through its cumulative and collaborative work since the 1970s has been to forge an "invigorated" space within the "invited" space of the discipline of biblical studies, even within the Biblical Studies academy of the Euro-American axis.[75] Within the Third World forms of CBI have even constructed the "invented" space of a transformed "biblical studies" discipline,[76] such as the recently constructed "Bible and Social Change" discipline at the University of KwaZulu-Natal, South Africa, the "biblical studies" work being done in Asia-Pacific contexts, and through the cross-generational collaborative and disruptive biblical studies work associated with the "Discernment and Radical Engagement" (DARE) forum of the Council for World Mission, which like the Circle commits itself to the curation of a publication archive of reception-context-based biblical scholarship.[77]

Accountable to contexts of reception and responsible to contextual contours of production

What makes the various forms of CBI "biblical" is that even while deconstructing and reconstructing—re-inventing[78]—biblical studies as a discipline, CBI retains a sense of responsibility to the biblical texts and their contexts of production. As already indicated, early forms of community-based CBI drew on socially engaged biblical scholarship which, though reception oriented, required an overt engagement with the contexts of the Bible's production.[79] Forms of CBI always engage with particular details of the biblical text, whether socio-historical, literary-narrative, or thematic-semiotic (to return

74 Havea, ed., *Talanoa ripples*; Vaka'uta, ed., *Talanoa rhythms*; Havea, ed., *Sea of readings*; Havea, ed., *Pacific well-being*.

75 Segovia and Tolbert, eds., *Social location and biblical interpretation in the USA*; Segovia and Tolbert, eds., *Social location and biblical interpretation in global perspective*; Wimbush and Rodman, *African Americans and the Bible*; Bailey, Liew, and Segovia, eds., *They were all*; Fiorenza, *Feminist*; Webster, "A Miner"; Boase and Frechette, eds., *Bible*; Hall, *Insights*; Moore, *Decolonial*; Ekblad, *Reading*; Dykstra and Myers, *Liberating*.

76 These analytical concepts are central to recent CBS analysis within the Ujamaa Centre and are elaborated in Zwane, "Invited"; West, Zwane, and Carlos, "Contending."

77 Havea, ed., *Scripture*; Choi and Rieger, *Faith*; Havea, *Dissension*.

78 Moore and Sherwood, *Invention*.

79 Schwantes, "Profecia e estado"; Fiorenza, *Bread*; Mosala, *Biblical*; Gottwald, *Hebrew*.

to Lategan's typology). The biblical text has a voice alongside the voices of readers, hearers, and users.

As I come towards the end of my article I should say something about my use of the term "users" of the Bible. I use this term to include the various contextual appropriations of the Bible as a sacred and powerful object, before it is even opened.[80] This dimension of biblical reception engages with might be called the materiality of the Bible, and has been reflected on within biblical scholarship across a range of contexts, particularly from the perspective of indigenous appropriations of the missionary-colonial Bible.[81] The sacred materiality of the Bible as a component of its production should be considered among the contextual dimensions of the Bible itself.

In his contribution to an African-European conversation about contextual biblical interpretation, South African Louis Jonker helpfully distinguishes three "contexts" of biblical reception: interpretive contextuality, didactic contextuality, meta-theoretical contextuality; and four "contexts" of biblical production: productive contextuality, rhetorical contextuality, literary contextuality, and canonical contextuality.[82] CBI, while explicitly or implicitly oriented to contexts of reception, always engages with at least one of the Bible's contexts of production. The discipline of "biblical studies" is changing, and CBI has played a role in this change, but the biblical text retains its "textual" integrity, whether as a socio-historical reconstruction or as a literary-narrative story or as a thematic-semiotic reservoir (or as an object of sacred power).[83] Particular biblical contextual detail is a critical component of each form of CBI, though different forms of CBI place a particular emphasis on particular kinds of production detail.

Conceptualizing contextual biblical interpretation

Fortunately for this emerging sub-discipline within Biblical Studies, CBI has been diligent in conceptualizing its work, combining actual context-based biblical interpretation with careful theoretical and methodological

80 West, "Open and closed."

81 Adamo, "Psalms"; Hamling, "Living"; West, *Stolen Bible*; Hidalgo, *Revelation*; Gampiot, *Kimbanguis*.

82 Jonker, "Living," 110–11.

83 Lategan, "Current," 14–6.

reflection. Most of the work cited in my article includes elements of reflection on a particular form of CBI. This established body of scholarship is the reason CBI has become established as a sub-discipline within the traditional Euro-American discipline of Biblical studies and as a form of biblical studies within its own right in the Third World, Global South, and margins of the Euro-American academy.

There is a host of postgraduate work being done within the family of CBI forms,[84] which requires careful documenting and analysis. The established hubs of CBI, including CEBI, the Ujamaa Centre, and CCBI, have generated an array of postgraduate research, including research which pushes the boundaries of CBI practice. For example, CBS has been used in Taiwan among the indigenous peoples both as a form of Bible translation and as a resource for recovering indigenous pre-colonial culture,[85] and in Ghana CBS has been used as a postcolonial form of Bible re-translation.[86]

There has also been work which intersects, for example, the work of CEBI and the work of the Ujamaa Centre,[87] as there has been work which intersects CBS and intercultural biblical interpretation.[88] In January 2015 a significant intersectional workshop was jointly hosted by CEBI (Brazil) and the Ujamaa Centre (South Africa), in partnership with Kerk in Actie (the Netherlands), "Networking 'Contextual Bible Reading' Project: Structures of Violence," held in Bogotá, Colombia. The purpose of the workshop in Colombia was, as the title suggests, a way of networking those who were doing forms of contextual biblical interpretation, using the term preferred by Kerk in Actie, "contextual Bible reading."

There were four layers of participants among the forty participants who came from Colombia, Guatemala, Brazil, Costa Rica, the USA, Scotland, the Netherlands, India, Cameroon, Kenya, and South Africa. The primary layer was those who had been formed by the liberation struggles in Brazil and South Africa (and related contexts, mostly notably the Philippines) in the 1970s and 1980s whose forms of contextual Bible reading where shaped by these political-economic struggles.[89] The second layer were those who had no direct relationship with the social movements of the 1970s and

84 See for example Curtis, "Re-reading"; Sødal, *Tause*; Lines, *Beyond eclecticism*; Webster, *When the Bible*; Pacheco Lozano, *Towards*; Yalamu, *Attempting*.

85 Chang, *Convocation House*.

86 Esala, "Translation."

87 West, "Relationship"; Nürnberger, *I will send*; Wittenberg, *I have heard*; Wittenberg, *Prophecy*.

88 Van der Walt, *Communal Reading*; West, "Locating"; López, "Contextual Bible reading."

89 Institute for Contextual Theology, *Road*.

1980s, but who had some experience in this liberation theology form of contextual Bible reading and who had some connection to organisations or movements of contextual biblical interpretation, usually either CEBI or the Ujamaa Centre. The third layer were individuals, most of them young social activists, who had little experience of CBI but who wanted to become practitioners of CBI and a part of CBI networks. And the fourth layer included a range of participants, including some academics who wanted to understand these forms of contextual biblical interpretation and some practitioners engaged in other forms of contextual biblical interpretation. Among this last category of participants were those who had extensive experience in the forms of CBI associated with Casitas Bíblicas (the "Bible house") movement, Colectivo Ecuménico de Biblistas (CEDEBI), and intercultural biblical interpretation.

This diversity of participation required regular clarification of the forms of "contextual Bible reading" being experienced through this workshop. But as this was a process driven workshop, theoretical and methodological clarification were not the first moment of the workshop. The workshop was structured within a See-Judge-Act process, the process integral to the contextual biblical interpretation praxis of both CEBI and the Ujamaa Centre.[90] Each of the three components (See-Judge-Act) was itself imbedded in a sharing of our local spiritualities and in corporate spiritual formation together, for most forms of CBI are situated within an infrastructure of faith.[91] The "See" component began with a recognition and sharing of our different realities. The second, third, and fourth day were dedicated to particular experiences of CBI, as part of the process of the "Judge" moment within the See-Judge-Act process. The workshop offered four in-depth experiences with four different, yet related, forms of CBI. The first was intercultural biblical interpretation which had been practised in Colombia, including a number of local Colombian participants from this project. The second was a visit to number of the Casitas Bíblicas located on the outskirts of Bogotá. The third was the Contextual Bible Study (CBS) form of contextual Bible reading of the Ujamma Centre from South Africa, and the fourth was da Leitura Popular da Bíblia form of contextual Bible reading practised by CEBI.

In each case workshop participants were given the opportunity to participate in and so experience each of these forms of contextual Bible reading before being offered analysis of the theoretical and methodological

90 West, "Reading"; see also Justin Sands, "Introducing."

91 West, "Contextual."

scaffolding of each of these forms. The experience of these different forms of contextual Bible reading generated a host of questions among participants, and so the morning of the final day, as the workshop was moving into the "Act" moment, was given over to theoretical and methodological reflection. In preparation for this conceptual "clearing" and clarification, CEBI and the Ujamaa Centre met to draft a joint presentation, recognizing as we have for more than thirty-five years that our theoretical and methodological "commitments" were very similar. We agreed that it was important to clarify the "political" (to use CEBI's term) or "ideological" (to use Ujamaa's term) "values" which shaped our forms of CBI.

As we discussed our core values together, across different languages, we drew on the long conceptual conversations that have characterized our work, much of which has been referenced in this article. Within the praxis of CEBI there were five core values, one for each finger of a hand. Within the literature of Ujamaa there were four or five core "commitments."[92] This workshop gave CEBI and the Ujamaa Centre an opportunity, as we had intended, both to learn from each other and others, and to consolidate our reflections on our practices. As we talked together we discerned that our various core value categories could be consolidated in the form of five "C's" (for pedagogical purposes): Community, Criticality, Collaboration, Change, and Context. We also agreed, among those present, that there was a sixth "C," Contestation. This sixth "C" was already a core value of the Ujamaa Centre's work, but had not yet formed a component value of CEBI's self-understanding, but had been a matter of debate among CEBI practitioners. We decided to include this sixth "C" in our presentation. In recent reflection the Ujamaa Centre has attempted to weave these six non-negotiable core values into a coherent contextual shape that guides our CBI praxis: CBS begins with the realities of particular local communities of the poor and marginalized [Community], working together in the organized structures and spaces they have established and control [Criticality], collaborating with each other and the socially engaged biblical scholars and theologians who are already working with them [Collaboration] for social transformation [Change], and whom they have invited to read the Bible with them [Collaboration], communally and critically making use of biblical studies resources [Criticality], within particular local contextual struggles [Context] for particular emancipatory outcomes [Change], recognising that the Bible is both a community-building resource [Change] and itself a site of ideo-theological contestation [Contestation]. We agreed too on a seventh

92 West, *Contextual*; Nadar, "Liberation Discourse"; Nadar, "Hermeneutics."

value: Celebration! The relentless process of See-Judge-Act, See-Judge-Act, [...] must embrace moments of celebration as we recognise God's transforming work through CBI.

This discussion of the core values which shape CBI is important because it reflects a concern shared by both CEBI and the Ujamaa Centre that our forms CBI are not formulaic "methods" or "techniques." It is for this reason that CEBI has been so hesitant to produce a training "manual." Instead, they offer "popular education" praxis interpretive models or methods discerned within the Bible, the most well-used being "the walk to Emmaus,"[93] alongside others like "The Evangelist and the Minister Meet on the Road" (Acts 8:26-40), "Encounters of Dialogue between the Samaritan Woman and Jesus" (John 4:3-42), and "Parables: Histories of Life Pregnant with Mystery."[94]

The Ujamaa Centre too was hesitant to produce a training manual, worrying that CBS would become formulaic, rather than a political-ideological faith-full praxis. As indicated, CBS is usually scaffolded within a spirituality of liberation and follows the shape of the six Cs above. However, while working with students from the Gurukul Theological College and Research Institute, Chennai, India, in 2003 and 2005, the Ujamaa Centre was persuaded to provide a resource manual. The first edition of the Ujamaa Centre's "Doing Contextual Bible Study: A Resource Manual" was produced in 2005 and revised each year until 2015.[95] Early forms of this "manual" have been used by many other "manuals" since.[96] The revisions have been generated by the action-reflection praxis that is integral to CBS.

The presence of actual local community-based readers, hearers, and users of the Bible within the kinds of CBI work practised by CEBI and the Ujamaa Centre, often with a particular organized group over extensive periods of time, generates regular action-reflection cycles as part of their respective See-Judge-Act processes. The Ujamaa Centre's work in the context of HIV is a good example,[97] as is our work in the context of LGBTIQA+ sexualities.[98] The kind of reflection evident in CEBI's historical overview offers a similar insight into how the action-reflection cycle shapes a CBI

93 Dreher, *Walk*; West, "Do Two Walk Together?"; Anglican Communion, *God's justice*.

94 Schinelo, *Bible*, 29–36, 37–44, and 45–56; see also Nadar, Ueti, and Jodamus, "Gender justice."

95 Ujamaa, *Doing*.

96 See for example Martinsen, Nielsen, and Kiil Saga, *Tekster*; Moyo, *Biblical Journey*; Ujamaa, *Doing*; Fecclaha, *Tamar*; Tearfund, *Hand*; Makoka and West, *Health-promoting*; Anglican Alliance and Ujamaa Centre, *Re-imagining*; Colgan and Blyth, eds., *Accompanying*.

97 West, "Senzeni na?"

98 West, Van der Walt, and Zwane, "Boundaries."

praxis.[99] While it is clear that organized actual local community-based readers, hearers, and users of the Bible summon the cycle of action-reflection, it is not clear whether those forms of CBI associated with mainstream biblical studies, which have an implied-indirect rather an explicit-direct presence of actual local community-based readers, hearers, and users of the Bible, experience the same summons to participate in regular cycles of action-reflection.

However, what warrants the inclusion of these many Third World or Global South or margins of the Euro-American mainstream forms of contextual biblical interpretation as participating in a form of action-reflection is that not only do they have an actual local context-based real reader as an implied dialogue partner, they submit themselves as socially engaged biblical scholars to scholarly dialogical processes, ensuring that their particular form of CBI does participate in forms of reflection. We can think here, for example, of the annual meetings of the African Biblical Hermeneutics section within the Society of Biblical Literature, where there is a regular invitation to participants to reflect on theory and method.[100] The regular volumes of *Revista Teológica de la Universidad Bíblica Latinoamericana* and the related *Vida y Pensamiento* offer similar sites for theoretical, methodological, and conceptual reflection within the Latin American region.[101] Similarly, the meetings of Talanoa Oceania every two years also generate regular reflection on Asia-Pacific contextual biblical interpretation across regions and generations, including an overtly *Kautaha* (collaboration) component.

The empirical orientation of interculturation biblical interpretation and the research of the CCBI has invited its own regular reflection,[102] offering CBI the opportunity to reflect on the continuum ranging from empirical research forms of CBI to action-reflection forms of CBI.[103] Other empirical forms of biblical studies, documenting how the Bible is interpreted, for example, by African political leaders within the public realm,[104] though they contribute to a community of socially engaged biblical scholars, do not envisage a dialogical work with these readers, and so should probably

99 Míguez, "Latin American"; Schinelo, *Bible*, 57–66.

100 See for example Masenya, Høyland Lavik, and Dykesteen Nilsen, eds., *Context*. See also the SBL related series Bailey, Liew, and Segovia, *They Were All*; Liew and Segovia, *Reading biblical texts*; Liew and Segovia, eds., *Reading in these times*.

101 See for example Sandoval, "El libro."

102 See for example Segovia, "Intercultural."

103 Van der Walt, *Communal Reading*; Forster, *(Im) possibility*; López, "Contextual Bible reading."

104 Gunda, *On the public role*.

not be included within the CBI family. However, research projects like the "Bible in the Life of the Church," which in the wake of irresponsible sexuality-related uses of the Bible in the 1998 Lambeth Conference attempted to document how ordinary Anglicans within the Anglican Communion actually read their Bibles, should be included. Such work anticipates forms of documentation and analysis, offering resources for cross-Communion forms of biblical interpretation.[105]

Conclusion

It is appropriate to conclude my article with the question of the extent of the extended family of CBI. I have erred on inclusion, arguing that it is a useful hermeneutic exercise to reflect on how various forms of CBI are or might be related to one another in a variety of different ways. My impulse to include is warranted when one considers the recently published edited volume *Challenging Contextuality: Bibles and Biblical Scholarship in Context*,[106] within which almost all the forms of CBI I have referenced are included. But the diverse forms of CBI do not usually collect themselves into convenient edited volumes, so the kind of conceptual and archival work in this article offers a first step in what is envisaged as a yearly overview of the discipline.

I have identified a number of conceptual parameters of CBI. First, CBI includes biblical studies work in which the context of biblical reception is the subject of interpretation. Second, CBI recognises that the context of reception is an inhabited or peopled context and these actual local context-based people are the subjects of interpretation. While my own preferred forms of CBI are those that involve an actual embodied presence of the subjects of interpretation, I recognize a kindred connection with forms of CBI where socially engaged biblical scholars have an implied dialogue with actual context of reception readers. Third, the different forms of CBI each include a commitment to forms of social and theological transformation. Biblical interpretation should contribute to change of the context of reception. Fourth, the various forms of CBI, while accountable to reception context-based readers are each "biblical" in that they may use of the resources of biblical studies, while challenging and changing the discipline. Fifth, CBI contributes to the changing of the discipline

105 Lyon, "Mind the gap!"; see also Village, *Bible*.
106 Lawrence et al., eds., *Challenging*.

of biblical studies through its careful conceptual work, creating communities of theoretical and methodological reflection within forms of action-reflection praxis.

The bibliography which follows is comprehensive of the different kinds of CBI reflected on in this article, but each of the forms of CBI has a far more extensive body of scholarship.

Bibliography

Adamo, David Tuesday. "The Use of Psalms in African Indigenous Churches in Nigeria." In *The Bible in Africa. Transactions, Trajectories and Trends*, edited by Gerald O. West and Musa Dube. Leiden: Brill, 2000, 336–49.

Anglican Alliance and Ujamaa Centre. "Re-Imagining Our World Together. Contextual Bible Studies on the Anglican Marks of Mission and the Sustainable Development Goals." Anglican Communion (2023). Accessed November 18, 2024. https://files.anglicanalliance.org/wp-content/uploads/2023/01/05100502/Re-imagining-our-World-Together-Contextual-Bible-Studies.pdf.

Anglican Communion. *God's Justice. Just Relationships between Women and Men, Girls and Boys. Study Materials for Use by Theological Colleges, Seminaries and Training Schemes in the Anglican Communion.* Accessed November 18, 2024. https://www.anglicancommunion.org/media/346995/acc17-study-materials-just-relationships.pdf.

Appiah-Kobi, Kofi, and Sergio Torres, eds. *African Theology En Route. Papers from the Pan-African Conference of Third World Theologians, December 17–23, 1977, Accra, Ghana.* Maryknoll, NY: Orbis Books, 1983.

Bailey, Randall C., Tat-siong Benny Liew, and Fernando F. Segovia, eds. *They Were All Together in One Place? Toward Minority Biblical Criticism.* Semeia Studies 57. Atlanta: SBL Press, 2009.

Boase, Elizabeth, and Christopher G. Frechette, eds. *Bible through the Lens of Trauma.* Semeia Studies 86. Atlanta: SBL Press, 2016.

Byron, Gay L., and Vanessa Lovelace. *Womanist Interpretations of the Bible. Expanding the Discourse.* Atlanta: SBL Press, 2016.

Chang, Wallis C. "A Convocation House (Prrngawan). Biblical Interpretation and Tycm Tribal Postcolonial Concerns. Reading Genesis 2:4b-25 with Tycm Ordinary Tribal Readers." PhD dissertation, University of KwaZulu-Natal, South Africa, 2012.

Choi, Jin Young, and Joerg Rieger. *Faith, Class, and Labor. Intersectional Approaches in a Global Context.* Eugene: Wipf and Stock Publishers, 2020.

Claassens, L. Juliana, Steed V. Davidson, Charlene van der Walt, and Ashwin Thyssen, eds. *Queering the Prophet. On Jonah and Other Activists*. Atlanta: SCM Press, 2023.

Claassens, L. Juliana, Christl M. Maier, and Funlola O. Olojede, eds. *Transgression and Transformation. Feminist, Postcolonial and Queer Biblical Interpretation as Creative Interventions*. London: T&T Clark, 2021.

Colgan, Emily, and Caroline Blyth, eds. *Accompanying Survivors of Sexual Harm. A Toolkit for Churches*. UK: The Shiloh Project, 2023.

Curtis, Andrew. "Re-Reading the Gospel of Luke Today. From a First Century Urban Writing Site to a Twentieth Century Urban Reading Site." PhD dissertation, Open University: UK, 1998.

Dreher, Carlos A. *The Walk to Emmaus*. São Leopoldo: Centro de Estudos Bíblicos, 2004.

Dube, Musa W., ed. *Other Ways of Reading. African Women and the Bible*. Atlanta: SBL Press, 2001.

Dube, Musa W., and Musimbi Kanyoro, eds. *Grant Me Justice! HIV/AIDS and Gender Readings of the Bible*. Pietermaritzburg: Cluster Publications, 2004.

Dube, Musa W., Andrew M. Mbuvi, and Dora R. Mbuwayesango. *Postcolonial Perspectives in African Biblical Interpretations*. Atlanta: SBL Press, 2012.

Dykstra, Laurel, and Ched Myers. *Liberating Biblical Study. Scholarship, Art, and Action in Honor of the Center and Library for the Bible and Social Justice*. Eugene: Cascade Books, 2011.

Ekblad, Bob. *Reading the Bible with the Damned*. Louisville: Westminister John Knox Press, 2005.

Esala, Nathan A. "Translation as Invasion in Post-Colonial Northern Ghana." PhD dissertation, University of KwaZulu-Natal, South Africa, 2021.

Fabella, Virginia, and Mercy Amba Oduyoye, eds. *With Passion and Compassion. Third World Women Doing Theology*. Maryknoll, NY: Orbis Books, 1988.

Fabella, Virginia, and Sergio Torres, eds., *Doing Theology in a Divided World* Maryknoll, NY: Orbis Books, 1985.

Fabella, Virginia, and Sergio Torres, eds. *Irruption of the Third World. Challenge to Theology. Papers from the Fifth International Conference of the Ecumenical Association of Third World Theologians, August 17–29, 1981, New Delhi, India*. Maryknoll, NY: Orbis Books, 1983.

Fecclaha. *Tamar Campaign. Contextual Bible Study Manual and Sermon Outlines on Gender Based Violence and Peace*. Nairobi: The Fellowship of Christian Councils and Churches in the Great Lakes and the Horn of Africa (FECCLAHA), 2017.

Fiorenza, Elisabeth Schüssler. *Bread Not Stone. The Challenge of Feminist Biblical Interpretation*. Boston: Beacon, 1984.

Fiorenza, Elisabeth Schüssler. *Feminist Biblical Studies in the Twentieth Century. Scholarship and Movement.* Atlanta: SBL Press, 2014.

Forster, Dion A. *The (Im) Possibility of Forgiveness. An Empirical Intercultural Bible Reading of Matthew 18.15-35.* Eugene: Wipf and Stock, 2019.

Frostin, Per. *Liberation Theology in Tanzania and South Africa. A First World Interpretation.* Lund: Lund University Press, 1988. Reprint, Pietermaritzburg: Cluster Publications & Ujamaa Centre, 2021.

Gampiot, Aurélien Mokoko. *Kimbanguism. An African Understanding of the Bible.* University Park: Penn State Press, 2017.

Gottwald, Norman K. *The Hebrew Bible in Its Social World and in Ours.* Atlanta: Scholars Press, 1993.

Gunda, Masiiwa Ragies. *On the Public Role of the Bible in Zimbabwe.* Bamberg: University of Bamberg Press, 2015.

Hall, Crystal L. *Insights from Reading the Bible with the Poor.* Minneapolis: Fortress Press, 2019.

Hamling, Tara. "Living with the Bible in Post-Reformation England. The Materiality of Text, Image and Object in Domestic Life." *Studies in Church History* 50 (2014): 210–39.

Havea, Jione. *Dissension and Tenacity. Doing Theology with Nerves.* Lanham: Lexington Books / Fortress Academic, 2022.

Havea, Jione, ed. *Pacific Well-Being. (Is)Lands, Theologies, Worldviews.* Eugene: Pickwick, 2024.

Havea, Jione, ed. *Scripture and Resistance.* New York and London: Lexington/ Fortress Academic, 2019.

Havea, Jione, ed., *Sea of Readings. The Bible in the South Pacific.* Atlanta: SBL Press, 2018.

Havea, Jione, ed. *Talanoa Ripples. Across Borders, Cultures, Disciplines.* Albany: Massey University, 2010.

Hidalgo, Jacqueline M. *Revelation in Aztlán. Scriptures, Utopias, and the Chicano Movement.* New York: Springer, 2016.

Institute for Contextual Theology. *The Road to Damascus. Kairos and Conversion.* Johannesburg: Skotaville, 1989.

Ipsen, Avaren. *Sex Working and the Bible.* London: Equinox, 2009.

Jonker, Louis C. "Living in Different Worlds Simultaneously, Or: A Plea for Contextual Integrity." In *African and European Readers of the Bible in Dialogue. In Quest of a Shared Meaning,* edited by Hans de Wit and Gerald O. West. Leiden: Brill, 2008, 105–19.

Lategan, Bernard. "Current Issues in the Hermeneutical Debate." In *Hermeneutics and Social Transformation. A Selection from the Essays of Bernard Lategan,* edited by Dirk J. Smit. Stellenbosch: Sun Press, 2015, 13–27.

Lawrence, Louise, Peter-Ben Smit, Hannah M. Strømmen, and Charlene van der Walt, eds. *Challenging Contextuality. Bibles and Biblical Scholarship in Context.* Oxford: Oxford University Press, 2024.

Liew, Benny Tat-siong, and Fernando F. Segovia, eds. *Reading in These Times. Contexts of Minoritized Biblical Criticism.* Semeia Studies 103. Atlanta: SBL Press, 2024.

Liew, Tat-siong Benny, and Fernando F. Segovia. *Reading Biblical Texts Together. Pursuing Minoritized Biblical Criticism.* Semeia Studies 98. Atlanta: SBL press, 2022.

Lines, Kevin P. "Beyond Eclecticism and toward Intercontextual Hermeneutics. Contextual Bible Study as a Model for Learning from Each Other," unpublished paper, Asbury Theological Seminary, 2009.

López, Edgar A. "Contextual Bible Reading and Intercultural Bible Reading. Four Colombian Experiences." *HTS Teologiese Studies/Theological Studies* 77:4 (2021): 1–8.

Lyon, Stephen. "Mind the Gap! Reflections on the Bible in the Life of the Church' Project." *Anglican Theological Review* 93:3 (2011): 449–62.

Mainwaring, Simon. *Mark, Mutuality, and Mental Health. Encounters with Jesus.* Atlanta: SBL Press, 2014.

Makoka, Mwai, and Gerald O. West. *Health-Promoting Churches. Contextual Bible Studies on Health and Healing.* Vol. III. Geneva: World Council of Churches, 2022. Accessed November 18, 2024. https://www.oikoumene.org/resources/publications/health-promoting-churches-volume-iii.

Martinsen, Anders, Jan Christian Nielsen, and Stine Kiil Saga. *Tekster Til Forandring. Et Bibelstudieopplegg.* Oslo: Verbum, 2010.

Masenya, Madipoane (Ngwan'a Mphahlele), Marta Høyland Lavik, and Tina Dykesteen Nilsen, eds. *Context Matters. Old Testament Essays from Africa and Beyond Honoring Knut Holter.* Atlanta: SBL Press, 2023.

Masenya, Madipoane Ngwan'a Mphahlele, and Kenneth N. Ngwa, eds. *Navigating African Biblical Hermeneutics. Trends and Themes from Our Pots and Our Calabashes.* Cambridge: Cambridge Scholars Publishing, 2018.

Mbuvi, Andrew M. "African Biblical Studies. An Introduction to an Emerging Discipline." *Currents in Biblical Research* 15:2 (2017): 149–78.

Mbuvi, Andrew M. *African Biblical Studies. Unmasking Embedded Racism and Colonialism in Biblical Studies.* London: Bloomsbury Publishing, 2022.

Melanchthon, Monica Jyotsna, and Robyn J. Whitaker, eds. *Terror in the Bible. Rhetoric, Gender, and Violence.* Atlanta: SBL Press, 2021.

Míguez, Néstor O. "Latin American Reading of the Bible. Experiences, Challenges and Its Practice." *Expository Times* 118:3 (2006): 120–29.

Mofokeng, Takatso. "Black Christians, the Bible and Liberation." *Journal of Black Theology* 2:1 (1988): 34–42.

Moore, Stephen D. *Decolonial Theory and Biblical Unreading. Delinking Biblical Criticism from Coloniality*. Leiden: Brill, 2024.

Moore, Stephen D., and Yvonne Sherwood. *The Invention of the Biblical Scholar. A Critical Manifesto*. Minneapolis: Fortress Press, 2011.

Mosala, Itumeleng J. *Biblical Hermeneutics and Black Theology in South Africa*. Grand Rapids: Eerdmans, 1989.

Mosala, Itumeleng J. "The Use of the Bible in Black Theology." In *The Unquestionable Right to Be Free. Essays in Black Theology*, edited by Itumeleng J. Mosala and Buti Tlhagale. Johannesburg: Skotaville, 1986, 175–99.

Moyo, Fulata Lusungu. *A Biblical Journey for Justice. Contextual Bible Studies*. Geneva: World Council of Churches, 2013.

Nadar, Sarojini. "Beyond the 'Ordinary Reader' and the 'Invisible Intellectual'. Shifting Contextual Bible Study from Liberation Discourse to Liberation Pedagogy." *Old Testament Essays* 22:2 (2009): 384–403.

Nadar, Sarojini. "'Hermeneutics of Transformation?' A Critical Exploration of the Model of Social Engagement between Biblical Scholars and Faith Communities." In *Postcolonial Perspectives in African Biblical Interpretations*, edited by Musa W. Dube, Andrew M. Mbuvi, and Dora Mbuwayesango. Atlanta: SBL Press, 2012, 389–406.

Nadar, Sarojini, Paulo Ueti, and Johnathan Jodamus. "Toward Gender Justice. Reimagining Religion, Race, Gender, and Sexuality in Acts 8: 26-40." *The Ecumenical Review* 75:1 (2023): 96–111.

Ngwa, Kenneth N. *Let My People Live. An Africana Reading of Exodus*. Louisville: Westminster John Knox Press, 2022.

Nürnberger, Margarete P. L.. ed. *I Will Send You to Pharaoh. Bible Studies on Exodus 1-15*. Pietermaritzburg: Institute for the Study of the Bible, 1992.

Okure, Teresa. "Feminist Interpretation in Africa." In *Searching the Scriptures. A Feminist Introduction*, edited by Elisabeth Schüssler Fiorenza. New York: Crossroads, 1993, 76–85.

Pacheco Lozano, Andres Felipe. "Towards a Theology of Reconciliation. A Pilgrimage of Justice and Peace to Heal Broken Relations in Colombia." PhD dissertation, Vrije Universiteit Amsterdam, the Netherlands, 2020.

Riches, John, Helen Ball, Roy Henderson, Craig Lancaster, Leslie Milton, and Maureen Russell. *What Is Contextual Bible Study? A Practical Guide with Group Studies for Advent and Lent*. London: SPCK, 2010.

Sandoval, Timothy J. "El Libro De Proverbios Y La Teología De La Prosperidad." *Vida y Pensamiento* 39:2 (2019): 109–47.

Sands, Justin. "Introducing Cardinal Cardijn's See–Judge–Act as an Interdisciplinary Method to Move Theory into Practice." *Religions* 9:129 (2018): 1–10.

Schinelo, Edmilson. ed. *The Bible and Popular Education. Encounters of Solidarity and Dialogue.* São Leopoldo: CEBI, 2009.

Schipani, Daniel S., Martien Brinkman, and Hans Snoek, eds. *New Perspectives on Intercultural Reading of the Bible. Hermeneutical Explorations in Honor of Hans De Wit.* Elkhart: Institute of Mennonite Studies, 2015.

Schwantes, Milton. "Profecia E Estado. Uma Proposta Para a Hermenêutica Profética." *Estudos Teológicos* 22:2 (1982): 105–45.

Segovia, Fernando F. "Intercultural Bible Reading as Transformation for Liberation. Intercultural Hermeneutics and Biblical Studies." In *Bible and Transformation. The Promise of Intercultural Bible Reading,* edited by Hans de Wit and Janet Dyk. Atlanta: SBL Press, 2015, 19–51.

Segovia, Fernando F. "Reading-Across. Intercultural Criticism and Textual Posture." In *Interpreting Beyond Borders,* edited by Fernando F. Segovia. Sheffield: Sheffield Academic Press, 2000, 59–83.

Segovia, Fernando F., and Mary Ann Tolbert, eds. *Reading from This Place. Social Location and Biblical Interpretation in the United States.* Vol. 1. Minneapolis: Fortress Press, 1995.

Segovia, Fernando F., and Mary Ann Tolbert, eds. *Reading from This Place. Social Location and Biblical Interpretation in Global Perspective.* Vol. 2. Minneapolis: Fortress Press, 1995.

Sødal, Jan Bjarne. "Tause Tungers Tale. Om Myndiggjørende Bibellesning Og Teologen Som Tilrettelegger Med Utgangspunkt I En Sørafrikansk Kontekst." Postgraduate thesis, University of Oslo, Norway, 2000.

Tearfund. *Hand in Hand Bible Studies to Transform Our Response to Gender-Based Sexual Violence.* Teddington: Tearfund, 2015.

Trible, Phyllis. "Depatriarchalization in Biblical Interpretation." *Journal of the American Academy of Religion* 41 (1973): 30–49.

Trible, Phyllis. *Texts of Terror. Literary-Feminist Readings of Biblical Narratives.* Philadelphia: Fortress, 1984.

Ujamaa. *Doing Contextual Bible Study. A Resource Manual.* Pietermaritzburg: Ujamaa Centre, 2015. Accessed November 18, 2024. http://ujamaa.ukzn.ac.za/RESOURCES_OF_UJAMAA/MANUAL_STUDIES.aspx.

Ukpong, Justin S. "Bible Reading with a Community of Ordinary Readers." In *Interpreting the New Testament in Africa,* edited by Mary Getui, Tinyiko S. Maluleke and Justin S. Ukpong. Nairobi: Acton, 2001, 188–212.

Ukpong, Justin S. "Developments in Biblical Interpretation in Africa. Historical and Hermeneutical Directions." In *The Bible in Africa. Transactions, Trajectories and Trends*, edited y Gerald O. West and Musa W. Dube. Leiden: E.J. Brill, 2000, 11–28.

Vaage, Leif E., ed. *Subversive Scriptures. Revolutionary Readings of the Christian Bible in Latin America*. Valley Forge: Trinity Press International, 1997.

Vaka'uta, Nasili, ed. *Talanoa Rhythms. Voices from Oceania*. Albany: Massey University, 2010.

van der Walt, Charlene. *Toward a Communal Reading of 2 Samuel 13*. Elkhart: Institute of Mennonite Studies, 2014.

Village, Andrew. *The Bible and Lay People. An Empirical Approach to Ordinary Hermeneutics*. Aldershot: Ashgate, 2007.

Webster, Tiffany. "'A Miner Knows Better Than Anybody You Have Little Power over Mother Nature'. Exploring Genesis 1: 26–31 and the Concepts of Control and Power with South Derbyshire Coal Miners." *Journal of the Bible and its Reception* 2:2 (2015): 145–74.

Webster, Tiffany. "When the Bible Meets the Black Stuff. A Contextual Bible Study Experiment." PhD dissertation, University of Sheffield, England, 2017.

Weems, Renita J. "Reading *Her Way* through the Struggle. African American Women and the Bible." In *Stony the Road We Trod. African American Biblical Interpretation*, edited by Cain Hope Felder. Minneapolis: Fortress Press, 1991, 57–77.

West, Gerald O. *Biblical Hermeneutics of Liberation. Modes of Reading the Bible in the South African Context.* 2nd revised edition. Maryknoll, NY and Pietermaritzburg: Orbis Books and Cluster Publications, 1995. Cluster Publications 1991.

West, Gerald O. *Contextual Bible Study*. Pietermaritzburg: Cluster Publications, 1993.

West, Gerald O. "Contextual Bible Study and/as Interpretive Resilience." In *That All My Live. Essays in Honour of Nyambura J. Njoroge*, edited by Ezra Chitando, Esther Mombo, and Masiiwa Ragies Gunda. Bamberg: University of Bamberg Press, 2021, 143–59.

West, Gerald O. "Contextual Bible Study as a Form of Contextual Theology. An Early Conceptual History." *Studia Historiae Ecclesiasticae* 48:2 (2022): 1–17.

West, Gerald O. "Do Two Walk Together? Walking with the Other through Contextual Bible Study." *Anglican Theological Review* 93:3 (2011): 431–49.

West, Gerald O. "Locating 'Contextual Bible Study' and Intercultural Biblical Hermeneutics within Biblical Liberation Hermeneutics." In *New Perspectives on Intercultural Reading of the Bible. Hermeneutical Explorations in Honor of Hans De Wit*, edited by Daniel S. Schipani, Martien Brinkman and Hans Snoek. Elkhart: Institute of Mennonite Studies, 2015, 107–35.

West, Gerald O. "The Open and Closed Bible. The Bible in African Theologies." In *African Christian Theologies in Transformation*, edited by Ernst M. Conradie. Stellenbosch: EFSA, 2004, 162–80.

West, Gerald O., ed. *Reading Other-Wise. Socially Engaged Biblical Scholars Reading with Their Local Communities*. Semeia Studies 62. Atlanta and Leiden: SBL Press and Brill, 2007.

West, Gerald O. "Reading the Bible with the Marginalised. The Value/S of Contextual Bible Reading." *Stellenbosch Theological Journal* 1:2 (2015): 235–61.

West, Gerald O. "Recovering the Biblical Story of Tamar. Training for Transformation, Doing Development." In *For Better, for Worse. The Role of Religion in Development Cooperation*, edited by Robert Odén and Tore Samuelsson. Halmstad: Swedish Mission Council, 2019, 153–65.

West, Gerald O. "The Relationship between Different Modes of Reading (the Bible) and the Ordinary Reader." *Scriptura* S9 (1991): 87–110.

West, Gerald O. "Senzeni Na? Speaking of God 'What Is Right' and the 'Re-Turn' of the Stigmatising Community in the Context of HIV". *Scriptura* 116:2 (2017): 260–77.

West, Gerald O. *The Stolen Bible. From Tool of Imperialism to African Icon*. Leiden and Pietermaritzburg: Brill and Cluster Publications, 2016.

West, Gerald O., and Musa W. Dube, eds. *Reading With: An Exploration of the Interface between Critical and Ordinary Readings of the Bible*. Semeia Studies 73. Atlanta: SBL Press, 1996.

West, Gerald O., and Thulani Ndlazi "'Leadership and Land'. A Very Contextual Interpretation of Genesis 37-50 in Kwazulu-Natal, South Africa." In *Genesis, Texts@Contexts*, edited by Athalya Brenner, Archie Chi Chung Lee, and Gale A. Yee. Minneapolis: Fortress Press, 2010, 175–190.

West, Gerald O., Sithembiso Zwane, and Charlene van der Walt. "From Homosexuality to Hospitality; from Exclusion to Inclusion; from Genesis 19 to Genesis 18." *Journal of Theology for Southern Africa* 168 (2021): 5–19.

West, Gerald O., Charlene van der Walt, and Sithembiso Zwane. "Boundaries of Biblical Scholarship and Queer Interventions." In *Oxford University Press Handbook of Bible, Race, and Diaspora*, edited by Mitzi J. Smith, Raj Nadella and Luis Menéndez-Antuña. Oxford: Oxford University Press, forthcoming.

West, Gerald O., and Sithembiso Zwane. "Re-Reading 1 Kings 21:1-16 between Community-Based Activism and University-Based Pedagogy." *Journal for Interdisciplinary Biblical Studies* 2:1 (2020): 179–207.

West, Gerald O., Sithembiso Zwane, and Helder L. Carlos. "Contending for Invented Space in African Context and Biblical Text. Intersecting Gender, Sexuality, Ethnicity and Economics." *Old Testament Essays* 36:3 (2023): 587–611.

West, Gerald O., Sithembiso Zwane, and Charlene van der Walt. "Resisting Interlocking Systems of Violence. The Ujamaa Centre's CBS Praxis." In *The Bible and Violence*, edited by Johanna Stiebert, Johnathan Jodamus, Chris Greenough, and Mmapula Kebaneilwe. London: Bloomsbury T&T Clark, forthcoming.

Wimbush, Vincent L., and Rosamond C. Rodman. *African Americans and the Bible. Sacred Texts and Social Textures*. New York: Continuum, 2000.

Wit, Hans de. *Empirical Hermeneutics, Interculturality, and Holy Scripture*. Elkhart, IN: Institute of Mennonite Studies, 2012.

Wit, Hans de. "Intercultural Hermeneutics." In *Through the Eyes of Another. Intercultural Reading of the Bible*, edited by Hans de Wit, Louis Jonker, Marleen Kool and Daniel Schipani. Elkhard, IN: Institute of Mennonite Studies and Vrije Universiteit, 2004, 477–92.

Wit, Hans de. "Through the Eyes of Another. Objectives and Backgrounds." In *Through the Eyes of Another. Intercultural Reading of the Bible*, edited by Hans de Wit, Louis Jonker, Marleen Kool and Daniel Schipani. Elkhard, IN: Institute of Mennonite Studies and Vrije Universiteit, 2004, 3–53.

Wit, Hans de, and Janet Dyk, eds. *Bible and Transformation. The Promise of Intercultural Bible Reading*. Semeia Studies 81. Atlanta: SBL Press, 2015.

Wit, Hans de, Louis Jonker, Marleen Kool, and Daniel Schipani, eds. *Through the Eyes of Another. Intercultural Reading of the Bible*. Amsterdam: Institute of Mennonite Studies, 2004.

Wit, Hans de, and Edgar Antonio López, eds. *The Widow and the Judge. Memory, Resistance, and Hope. Intercultural Reading of Luke 18.1–8 in Latin American Contexts of Impunity*. Amsterdam and Elkart: Foundation Dom Hélder Câmara Chair, VU University and Institute of Mennonite Studies, 2020.

Wit, Hans de, and Gerald O. West, eds. *African and European Readers of the Bible in Dialogue. In Quest of a Shared Meaning*. Leiden: Brill, 2008.

Wittenberg, Gunther H. *I Have Heard the Cry of My People. A Study Guide to Exodus 1–15*. Pietermaritzburg: Cluster Publications, 1992.

Wittenberg, Gunther H. *Prophecy and Protest. A Contextual Introduction to Israelite Prophecy*. Pietermaritzburg: Cluster Publications, 1993.

Wittenberg, Gunther H. *Resistance Theology in the Old Testament. Collected Essays*. Pietermaritzburg: Cluster Publications, 2007.

Wittgenstein, Ludwig. *Philosophical Investigations*. Translated by G.E.M. Anscombe. Oxford: Basil Blackwell, 1968.

Yalamu, Emmanuel Som. "Attempting an Inculturation Biblical Hermeneutics for an Indigenous Christian Community in Melanesia. A Critical Dialogue between the Molap Bible Readers and Romans 12:1–2, 9–21." PhD dissertation, University of Divinity, Australia, 2024.

Yong-Bock, Kim. *A Report of the First International Workshop on Bible Pedagogy. Popular Reading of the Bible*. Chonju, Korea: Hanil University & Theological Seminary 1997.

Zwane, Sithembiso S. "Invited, Invigorated and Invented Spaces. A Trans-Development Approach." In *Faith, Class, and Labor. Intersectional Approaches in a Global Context*, edited by Jin Young Choi and Joerg Rieger. Eugene: Pickwick Publications, 2020, 212–33.

Zwane, Sithembiso S. "Invited, Invigorated and Invented Spaces. An Analysis of the Ujamaa Centre's Ideotheological Conceptual Contribution to Participatory Community Development in South Africa and Beyond." PhD dissertation, University of KwaZulu-Natal, in progress.

Amsterdam University Press

YEARBOOK OF CONTEXTUAL BIBLICAL INTERPRETATION 1 (2024) 148-152
HTTPS://DOI.ORG/10.5117/YCBI2024.009.PAST

REVIEWS

Review of Sharon Betsworth and Julie Faith Parker, eds. *T&T Clark Handbook of Children in the Bible and the Biblical World*. T&T Clark Handbooks. London: T&T Clark, 2019. $207.00; ISBN: 9780567672575.

Laura Pasterkamp, PhD candidate Faculty Religion and Theology, Vrije Universiteit Amsterdam

In the past years an abundance of papers has been published about children and youth in biblical texts. Many of these are case-studies on particular texts and this is the main way in which scholars have contributed new material to the study field of children in the Bible and the biblical world. However, comprehensive compendiums with coherent methodologies and analyses of multiple texts or sources are sparse within this study field, and this *T&T Clark Handbook of Children in the Bible and the Biblical World* attempts to fill this gap by providing a collection of essays by different scholars on children and youth in the Hebrew Bible, the New Testament and other biblical texts. This is the first such compendium after *The Child in the Bible* by Marcia J. Bunge (ed.) was published in 2008. In *The Child in the Bible* several authors were brought together to write about topics surrounding child-characters in the Bible from varying perspectives. Most of these authors were not acquainted yet with this child-centred study of biblical texts. In the introduction of *T&T Clark Handbook of Children in the Bible and the Biblical World* Sharon Betsworth and Julie Faith Parkers state that "the goal of the book is to recognize the progress of the study of children in the biblical world in a relatively short amount of time and to guide continued work in the field ahead" (p. 1). The question is whether they were successful in completing this goal.

Child-centred research within biblical studies had its starting point in the late 1960s, but has really prospered from the 1990s onwards. In its infancy, the research focused mostly on finding the children in the biblical texts and biblical world and on aspects of children's formation. Following this phase, the research started focusing more on the relations of the children and the social worlds they were embedded in. Nowadays, the research is centred around children as active subjects. Most of the research within this latest stage has adopted a "childist perspective." This term was introduced into the field of biblical studies only in 2013.[1] The childist approach is a form of hermeneutics, building on the goals of feminism, that re-examines child-and youth characters in biblical texts. With this approach the child as a subject of the text, instead of a passive bystander, is put in the spotlight. By using this perspective to look at children in the texts anew, the interpreter challenges the assumptions about children's roles and experiences in society.[2] Most of the research that employs this "childist perspective" focuses on the child-character *an sich*, analysing only how the age and identity of a child influences the role of the character in a given text. However, sometimes an intersectional lens is added, researching not only the influence of age, but also of gender, social class, ethnicity, ablebodiedness, and other identity aspects of the children. Using this intersectional lense is crucial to recognise and respect the child character as a full human being with a complex identity.[3]

This handbook contains essays of varying authors, all with their own field of expertise. Because of this, the handbook offers an interdisciplinary overview of the research opportunities within the field of children in the biblical texts and world. The authors use different methodologies, taken from different study fields, ranging from narratology to archaeology, and from ethnology to biblical exegesis.

After the introduction, the book is divided into five sections: Orientation to the Field, Hebrew Bible, Intertextual Issues and Intertestamental Texts, New Testament, and Early Christian Apocrypha. With this structure this book thus follows a canonical order, which makes the book easy to follow and clear in its approach. The authors state that comparatively more research has been done on the New Testament than on the Hebrew Bible. Rather than trying to fill this gap by providing more research on children in the Hebrew Bible, this Handbook continues in that same vein, offering a bigger

1 Sharon Betsworth and Julie Faith Parker, "'Where Have All the Young Girls Gone?' Discovering the Girls of the Bible through Childist Analysis of Exodus 2 and Mark 5–7," *Journal of Feminist Studies in Religion* 38/2 (2022): 126.

2 Elkins, "Feminist Studies as the Mother of Childist Approaches to the Bible," in *Children and Method. Listening to and Learning from Children in the Biblical World*, ed. Kristine Hendriksen Garroway and John W. Martens (Leiden: Brill, 2020), 19–34.

3 See Kimberlé Crenshaw, "Demarginalizing the Intersection of Race and Sex. A Black Feminist Critique of Anti-discrimination Doctrine, Feminist Theory and Antiracist Politics," *University of Chicago Legal Forum* Vol. 1989 (1989): 139–67; Kimberlé, Crenshaw, *On Intersectionality. Essential Writings* (New York: New Press, 2017). Cf. Laura Pasterkamp, "Een jong meisje het zwijgen opgelegd? Een analyse vanuit een 'childist' perspectief van het slavenmeisje met de waarzeggende geest in Handelingen 16:16–18," *Kerk en Theologie* 74 (2023): 380–396.

section on the New Testament than on the Hebrew Bible. Within the New Testament, the Gospel of John, Acts, the Catholic Letters, and Revelation have had far less attention than other books. This is another gap is not filled, instead two of the chapters are dedicated to texts from 1 Corinthians.

The first section of the book, Orientation to the Field encompasses Chapters 2 and 3. In the second chapter Reidar Aasgaard provides an extensive outline of the research that has been done in the field of children in the Bible and biblical world, what has been lacking in past research, and the road scholars are taking currently within the field. It gives good incentives to start new projects to fill the gaps. The third chapter gives an overview of the varying interdisciplinary tools from other fields of study that could be used within "childist" biblical studies. The chapters lay out the potentials and drawbacks of the different tools, coming from fields like child psychology, childhood studies, children's literature, archaeology and others. The section on archaeology devotes too large of a part to the usage of burial rites for the identification of childhood phases. Although this gives considerable food for thought, the section could have benefitted from exploring the breadth of possibilities that archaeology offers for the study of children.

The second section of the book is dedicated to the Hebrew Bible. To start this section, Kristine Henriksen Garroway successfully introduces methodologies on how to find children in the Ancient Near East and the Hebrew Bible in the fourth chapter. The fifth chapter provides an interesting analysis of the texts and context about the sacrifice of firstborn children and the different ways of interpreting these. Dong Sung Kim looks critically at the formation of diaspora identities through the story of Esther in Chapter 6. Sadly, the author does not fully use the concept of Esther's supposed "childhood" versus Mordecai's adulthood in the analysis of his essay as much as one would expect from the introduction and the conclusion. Esther's childhood does not play much of a role in how the author interprets the texts, and neither do the ideas about childhood and enculturalisation that the author introduces earlier. Chapter 7 yields a good starting point for more research into children and youth in Proverbs. Julie Faith Parker shows in Chapter 8 that there is a world of possibilities for searching for children in the text using a "childist perspective." She includes three different ways of applying this perspective to texts. Because of this approach, the author is not able to go into depth with the latter two examples. This made the essay seem choppy and the analyses did not reach their full potential.

Chapters 9 and 10 are part of the third section on Intertextual Issues and Intertestamental Texts. Chapter 9 explores how trauma studies can give us new insights into the lives of children in the biblical world. There are a lot of possibilities by combining different lenses and perspectives with trauma studies, but the examples used in the text did not go beyond providing a mere foundation for further study. In the next chapter, Stephen M. Wilson writes about the coming-of-age story of Tobias in Tobit. His methodology is based on biblical studies, using different principles to aid in identifying the coming-of-age story. His methodology could have been made stronger by using principles from the study of children's literature and narratological analysis of children's stories, since coming-of-age stories are an important feature of this literature.

Chapters 11 to 15 form the section on the New Testament. The eleventh chapter on methodology is, like the one for the Hebrew Bible, a comprehensive overview of the possible methodologies. Chapter 12 successfully explores the parable of the children in the marketplace from a childist perspective by focusing on the role of the children and how they influence the purpose of the parable. In Chapter 13 Andy Lindeman Allen lays out a thought-provoking analysis of Luke 18:15–17 about the naming of children as "Proprietors of the Kingdom of God." This analysis could have richer if she applied a clear intersectional lens. The author of Chapter 14 brings to light how "gendered couplets" in Q, the designation used for material common to the Gospels of Matthew and Luke, have consequences for how to interpret the "household" references in the text. His final conclusion that this language, in which children can be detected, should be seen as metaphorical, was not entirely convincing. Surely, this language is a stylistic choice, nevertheless, even stylistic choices would be influenced by the contextual reality of the authors: what is said in the household texts probably would have reflected a part of their reality. Chapters 15 and 16 are both well-thought out analyses of texts from 1 Corinthians, using a childist perspective and the socio-historical context of these texts.

The last two chapters cover early Christian Apocrypha. The sixteenth chapter gives, although needed, a surface-level exploration of children that can be found in the apocryphal Acts. The intersectional lens which the author sets out to use in the introduction is not applied thoroughly. Varying identity aspects are mentioned, but not how these work together to influence the role of the characters in the texts. The author of Chapter 17 sums up the appearances of children in the apocryphal Infancy Gospels, but otherwise overlooks them and their unique experiences in flight and travel situations.

All of the authors of this Handbook aim to centre children in their texts. However, the useful "childist perspective" is not employed consistently, and the children and youth-characters that are supposed to be the focus of the research sometimes disappear into the background as passive actors. Moreover, the editors claim that "many of the authors also pay attention to issues of gender [...] in these ways, this book breaks new ground for the field" (p. 4). In a number of the essays, the intersectional lens, or focus on identity aspects like gender, completely overshadows the goal of centring the child in the texts. Attention is then fully given to the difference that gender makes for a particular character, which is undoubtedly important, but the influence of "being a child" on the character, their role, and experiences, is then ignored, and consequently the goal of the Handbook. In other essays the intersectional lens is only used on a surface-level, which does not do justice to the analysis of the characters in these texts.

Overall, this book provides an excellent starting point for students and researchers new to the field of children in the Bible and the biblical world, despite not being fully consistent with the application of the childist perspective and intersectional lens. This Handbook is an especially helpful guide in providing useful methodologies, a history of the research field, and new research prospects. Thus, the Handbook ultimately fullfills the goal that is formulated by the editors in the Introduction.

Amsterdam University Press
YEARBOOK OF CONTEXTUAL BIBLICAL INTERPRETATION 1 (2024) 153-157
HTTPS://DOI.ORG/10.5117/YCBI2024.010.SPRO

Review of Margaret Murray Talbot, *Why Jephthah's Daughter Weeps: A Child-Oriented Interpretation*. Biblical Interpretation Series, 199. Leiden and Boston: Brill 2022; Pages: xiv, 226 pp.; ISBN: 978-90-04-50817-0.

Prof. dr. Klaas Spronk, Retired professor of Old Testament at the Protestant Theological University, Utrecht

This well-written book is based on a PhD completed at the Brite Divinity School (Fort Worth, Texas) in 2020. It was presented in part at the annual SBL conference that year in her paper entitled "Agency and Assemblages: Assessing Bat-Yiphtach's Bleeding Body," which gives an indication of the answer to the question in the book's title. The author presents an entirely new interpretation of Judg. 11:38 as referring not to the virginity of Jephthah's daughter and her remaining childless, but to her first experience of her menstrual cycle (menarche) and the fact that she has "no agency to control her own bleeding body" (p. 185). This book can also be read as an introduction to child-focused studies in general and child-focused biblical scholarship in particular. This takes up more than half of the book and, in my opinion, adds more to the value of this book than the exegetical speculations.

In the dedication at the beginning of the book (p. v) the author shares her experience of "the grave harm and costs to children (and our later selves) caused by the community's doctrines, rituals, stories and words that no longer have meaning—or that need new meaning." The present study is for her "a chance to make new meanings and new community, gathered around the wisdom, humour, and curiosities in these ancient myths." The ancient story of the nameless daughter of judge Jephthah—Talbot names her Bat-Yiphtach—is taken up first to give her "significance as a child who matters" (p. 1), and then to show that "the theoretical lenses in childhood studies [...] offer critical views for questioning what previous interpretations have not questioned."

Of primary importance to this approach is that Talbot fills in gaps in the story in which the reader is not informed of, among other things, the age of the girl and the presence of a mother. For her child-focused interpretation she assumes that the girl is "a transitional, menstruating (post-menarcheal) child" (p. 7). This is very different from, as she remarks, the usual feminist approach which tends to see her as an adult woman and emphasises her role in opposition to male dominance. Talbot does not want to go along in this "adult-centric gender binary." In the review of previous scholarship in Chapter 2 she demonstrates that in the history of interpretation, most of the attention has been given to religious matters concerning the vow or to attempts at reconstructing the historical background. Talbot concludes that the ambiguity of the story allows for a multiplicity of interpretations and that she is the first to offer the characterisation of the girl as a child in transition and to suggest an interpretation through a child-focused lens. One question that remains after reading the following chapters is whether this really sheds new light on the ancient story. Has it not created a different new story about an in itself relevant topic, instead of recovering something that lay hidden in the old narrative?

Chapter 3 gives a good overview of child-oriented scholarship with very useful information about the state of the art, terminology, and the relation between child studies and biblical studies, both historical and literary. An important element for Talbot is that we as modern readers should question our clear-cut ideas about children and adulthood. "Querying (and queering) the presuppositions underlying and sustaining a child-adult binary is crucial in childhood studies" (p. 66). This is especially true for children like Jephthah's daughter in a different time and place.

In Chapter 4 Talbot, finally, explains why according to her Jephthah's daughter can be regarded as a transitional child lamenting her first menstrual cycle. Here too, she finally (p. 103, n. 3) explains what precisely she means with the often-used term "menarche." A basic argument for her thesis is derived from the ongoing discussion about the meaning of the Hebrew word *betulim*, usually translated as "virginity" in the phrases where the daughter of Jephthah asks permission to go away for two months "to bewail my virginity" (Judg. 11:37) and the subsequent report that indeed "she and her female companions bewailed her virginity" (verse 38). She notes that in the *Dictionary of Classical Hebrew* (Vol. 2, p. 289) David Clines has constructed a broad lexical domain *Batul*, which includes "young womanhood" and "virginity" and gives as the general meaning of *betulah* "young woman, esp. as marriageable, sometimes specific virgin." Nevertheless, the *DCH* maintains the traditional interpretation of *betulim* in Judges 11. Talbot finds more room for her interpretation in the study by Gordon Wenham[1]

1 Gordon Wenham, "*B^etûlāh* 'A Girl of Marriageable Age,'" *Vetus Testamentum* 22 (1972) 326–48.

in which he states that in some texts *betulim* should be taken to refer to the age and marks of adolescence, and not to virginity. Referring to Judg. 11:37-38 Wenham states that

> 'Virginity' or 'youth' would be equally appropriate translations here, but the sad tale ends on a note, whose full pathos is only apparent if it is an additional piece of information, "She had never known a man" (v. 39) (p. 341; quoted by Talbot on p. 111, n. 33).

In his opinion it would be pointless to add this information if it was clear that the word *betulim* had no meaning other than "virginity." It should be noted, however, that Wenham still interprets this text within the framework of virginity and childbearing. Talbot clearly goes in a different direction when she concludes that *betulim* "might indicate actual experience and concern with transitioning female children and how they navigate the outward and inwards effects of change during their pubescence" (p. 112). It is a weak basis for the exegetical exposition that follows.

Before—as she rightly calls it on p. 128—she goes on to "construct" a child-oriented interpretation of Judg. 11:29-40, Talbot gives a very instructive overview of biblical scholarship on menstruation and on adolescence and menarche in childhood studies. With regard to the latter, it is remarkable that she relies primarily on "majority world cultural contexts," for example on young girls in Nepal and Tanzania, avoiding the danger of "colonial imperialism" in applying "minority world conceptualizations and priorities" (p. 129, n. 97). However politically correct this may be, this does not take away the risk that the gap between life in ancient Israel and life as it is experienced in our own times is bridged too easily.

The new approach to the story of Jephthah's daughter leads to a number of new interpretations. The first new element is found in the first verse. Talbot translates: "And upon Yiphtach was the *death-dealing* spirit of YHWH" (p. 163). This remarkable addition "death-dealing" is not related to the child-focused approach, but more generally with the fact that Talbot wants to leave "room for multiplicity," that is, alongside the common more constructive view of the spirit of the Lord in "a less sanguine, more violent sense" (p. 151, n. 188) as is demonstrated in the great smiting of the Ammonites reported in the following verses.

According to Talbot it is better not to take Mitspah as the name of a town, but to retain its original meaning of "watchtower" in 11:29. She combines the two as "watchtower in Mitspah" in 11:34. In this way she leaves open the possibility of a symbolic connection with menstruation as is found in folktales about nubile maidens locked away in towers, analogous to the custom of secluding menstruating women in many societies.

Talbot relates the phrase "only she alone" in verse 34, which is usually interpreted and translated as "she was his only child," to the phrase about her dancing and playing the tambourine: she would have come out dancing to meet her father all alone. This seems a rather forced attempt to stay away from the theme of Jephthah losing the prospect of progeny. Instead, Talbot wants to focus on the girl as a child in transition with few relationships, assuming that she is part of a far from perfect household, that also lacks a mother.

Talbot also attempts to relate the repeated reference to "two new moons" in verses 37–39 to menarche and menstruation. It could have been a euphemistic reference by the girl to her father that she had experienced menarche in his absence, or an indication that she first had to undertake a period of menstrual separation before she could return to him to be sacrificed.

An important element in this interpretation from the perspective of the daughter is her lack of agency. This is discussed in Chapter 5 on "Relational Assemblages and Bat-Yiphthach's Agency." This is introduced with a useful introduction to the topic in child-related studies. Here she draws on theories of childhood by sociologists Nick Lee, David Oswell, and Michael Gallagher, whose research constructs agency relationally and contextually in open assemblages. She goes against the trend among modern interpreters to emphasise her autonomous stance in relation to her father. Jephthah's daughter is at the mercy of her body (she bleeds), her father (she echoes his words and obeys), and socio-cultural and religious traditions for menstruating girls (her father tells her "to go" in verse 38).

The book ends in the final chapter with "Conclusions [...] and more questions." Talbot notes three "opportunities for future research." The first is the interpretation of the "two months" and the possible relation to ancient mythologies that connect menstrual and lunar cycles. The second is the question of whether the focus on children in transition can be also useful in the interpretation of other narratives in the book of Judges. Thirdly and more generally the narrative of Jephthah and his daughter read in this way, may stimulate "posing questions about the degree to which cultic norms and interpretations of previous (priestly) generations regarding the 'right' in the deity's eyes are indeed still right" (pp. 200-201). It is especially important to question the presuppositions that underlie the common child-adult binary.

After reading this book one may be stimulated to adopt a child-oriented approach in the interpretation of biblical texts. When it comes to the way Talbot applies it to the narrative of Jephthah and his daughter, most readers will probably be less convinced of the value of its results. Too much depends on the hypothetical suggestion about the physical condition of the daughter. When Talbot considers the scholarship on the girl and laments that it "fails to account for the menstrual bleeding" (p. 146) she suggests that this aspect has remained hidden in the text until now. Instead, it is more to the point that she uses the story to bring up the theme of menarche and the agency of a menstruating young girl. This is in itself an important topic related to questioning the adult-child binary, and is something that is added to this story in order to make it a topic of discussion.

For the interpretation of the book of Judges it is certainly useful to look at it from the perspective of children, but not in the way Talbot suggests. Recurring themes are those of having progeny, and the relationship between parent and child. This can easily be illustrated by the storyline in its literary context, ignored by Talbot. The story of Jephthah and his daughter is preceded by the story of Gideon who declined the offer to start a dynasty with his son as his successor on the throne (Judg. 8:23). Shortly before that we read about his young son Jeter, who does not dare to kill a captive enemy (8:20). Later, Gideon names another son Abimelek, which can be translated as "my father is king." This contradicts Gideon's earlier decision about kingship within the family. This son Abimelek turns out to be a disastrous leader. After Abimelek we hear of two judges, the second of whom has no less than thirty sons (10:4). This is in sharp contrast with Jephthah who has only one child. He is followed by three judges, two of whom again stand out because of their numerous offspring. The first has thirty sons and thirty daughters (12:9), the third has forty sons and thirty grandsons (12:14). In the next story progeny is again problematic. It begins with an elaborate narrative about a childless couple who eventually after divine intervention, receive Samson as their son. It can be seen as a counterpart to the story of Jephthah who loses his only child after dubious negotiations with God. It is also interesting to compare the conversation between Jephthah and his daughter with the conversations between Samson and his parents.

The book concludes with an extensive bibliography (very useful, especially for those interested in childhood studies), indices of modern authors (indicating that not all the literature mentioned in the bibliography is actually used), subjects, and scriptural citations.

Colophon

The *Yearbook of Contextual Biblical Interpretation* offers an international, interdisciplinary, and innovative platform for scholarly research in the field of contextual Biblical interpretation. Embracing contextuality as a catalyst for interpretation, the Yearbook is dedicated to fostering interpretations of Biblical texts that contribute to the flourishing of both humanity and the broader ecological world. Each year, the publication focuses on a specific area of concern, around which invited contributions and open-call submissions are organized.

Uitgever
Amsterdam University Press
Nieuwe Prinsengracht 89
1018 VR Amsterdam
www.aup.nl

Bezoek voor het afsluiten van een abonnement onze website www.aup-online.com.
Zie voor meer informatie https://www.aup-online.com/content/30504937.

Wilt u op de hoogte blijven van het laatste nieuws en van interessante nieuwe artikelen en boeken op het gebied van religie of geschiedenis? Schrijf u dan nu in op de nieuwsbrief van AUP, via www.aup.nl.

Omslagontwerp: Coordesign, Leiden
Lay-out: Crius Group, Hulshout

ISSN 3050-4929 (print)
ISSN 3050-4937 (online)
ISBN 978 90 4856 860 4